THE
PURGIN
OF A
EVI

THE PURGING OF AN EVIL

Analysis of race relations in the United States
Comprehensive solution to the racial problem

Roger L. Brewer

R. L. Brewer Publications
Rockfall, Connecticut 1991

R. L. Brewer
P.O. Box 26
Rockfall, Connecticut 06481

Library of Congress Catalog Card Number: 91-91951

ISBN: 0-9628797-0-3

Printed in the United States of America

CONTENTS

INTRODUCTION

This book analyzes race relations in the United States and proposes a comprehensive solution to the racial problem. Yes, there is a solution.

We strive today in the fight against racial inequality to maintain and enforce laws and rules that prohibit racial discrimination. And we must certainly continue to prohibit discriminatory conduct. Discriminatory conduct, however, is but a symptom and not the source of our problem. The source of our problem is race-consciousness.

Race-consciousness results in the perception that blacks are different. And the perception that blacks are different results necessarily in discriminatory behavior. If you perceive blacks as being different you will treat them accordingly. Thus, race-consciousness precludes equality of treatment.

This book recommends that we discontinue all race-conscious practices, including black separatism, race-conscious remedies, and other race-conscious efforts. This book recommends that we strive to provide for all the people of our country, with special attention to the poor, without regard to matters of race.

Also, this book discusses the racial problem in the United States, not as it pertains to blacks or whites, but as it pertains to the American people. Our racial predicament is not a black or white problem. It is an American problem, and not on the basis alone of American morality. We are moving today as a nation in the direction of another era of racial turmoil, which would divide and preoccupy the American people, and impair us in our ability to attend to other important matters affecting our lives, including matters of great importance to the national security of the United States.

Part One:
The Problem

CHAPTER 1

TO THE DETRIMENT OF ALL

Prior to the American Civil War, the institution of slavery, which consisted basically of the enslavement of blacks, was without question both permitted and protected by state laws in many jurisdictions of our country. Southern states had strong economic, political and emotional ties to slavery. Abolitionists, on the other hand, found slavery offensive and wanted it destroyed.

Controversy over slavery motivated Southern states ultimately to withdraw from the Union. Southern states organized as the Confederate States of America and set up their own separate government. The object of the American Civil War, insofar as the United States was concerned, was to put down the insurrection, and not necessarily to abolish slavery. In a letter on August 22, 1862 to the Editor of the New York Tribune, President Abraham Lincoln wrote, "My paramount object in this struggle is to save the union, and it is not either to save or destroy slavery. If I could save the union without freeing any slave, I would do it; and if I could do it by freeing some and leaving others alone, I would also do that."[1] The President's Emancipation Proclamation, which became effective on January 1, 1863, was a military measure to weaken forces in rebellion. It was issued after the country was well into the war and freed slaves in rebellious states only.

The Civil War continued for a period of four years (from 1861 to 1865). The cost to the United States was approximately $15,000,000,000 and more than one million casualties (about 617,000 deaths and 500,000 wounded).[2]

Slavery was abolished following the Civil War by Constitutional Amendment. We did not act at that time as a nation, however, to prohibit other racially discriminatory practices. For nearly a century following the Civil War racial segregation was permitted by law, and in many jurisdictions even required by law, in practically every aspect of American life. The racial oppression of blacks was allowed to continue. Racial discrimination persisted in an open and notorious fashion.

The Civil Rights Movement of the 1950's and 1960's, which consisted essentially of a multitude of activities and endeavors employed throughout the United States to accomplish various anti-racist objectives, was a powerful effort against continuing racist practices.[3]

Sit-in campaigns were used during the late 1950's and early 1960's to desegregate public facilities and accommodations. Blacks (and also blacks and whites together) went into segregated places for service in defiance of local customs and laws prohibiting service to blacks. Black and white students became heavily involved in these activities. By September of 1961, more than 70,000 students had participated.

Public demonstrations were also used to challenge racist practices. People assembled in public places and expressed feelings and demands relative to segregation and other racial injustices. Public demonstrations were numerous and continuous and were most frequently used during the 1960's. In the year 1963 alone, there were more than 10,000 racial demonstrations in the United States and more than 5,000 blacks were arrested for their roles in civil rights activities. 1963 was the year also of the historic Civil Rights March on Washington, D.C. that involved approximately 250,000 people.

The Civil Rights Movement, which consisted additionally of school desegregation efforts, boycotts, voter registration drives and other anti-racist initiatives, was strongly and vehemently opposed by some racially motivated Americans. And the opposition to civil rights was frequently a matter of violence and intimidation.

Opposition to civil rights resulted in difficulty especially in efforts to desegregate public schools. Rioting broke out in 1956, for example, as a result of the admission of a black student to the University of Alabama. In 1957, a white mob threatened to lynch and do other harm to black students who integrated Central High School in Little Rock, Arkansas. The President of the United States was required to send in federal troops to maintain order. In 1958, an integrated high school in Clinton, Tennessee was blown up. Rioting developed in 1962 as a result of the admission of a black student to the University of Mississippi. The rioting at the University of Mississippi resulted in two deaths and injuries to one hundred others.

Violent opposition to civil rights extended to all anti-racist activity. In April of 1963, a white postman protesting segregation was shot to death near Attalla, Alabama. Civil rights leader Medgar Evers was shot to death in Jackson, Mississippi on June 12, 1963. Also in 1963, the bombing of a church in Birmingham, Alabama killed four black children and injured twenty-one others. In 1964, Michael Schwerner, James Chaney and Andrew Goodman were killed by whites in Mississippi for their civil rights efforts. Civil rights worker Viola Liuzzo was shot to death in Alabama on March 25, 1965. On January 3, 1966, a black college student was killed in Tuskegee, Alabama for attempting to use a rest room reserved for whites only. Civil rights leader Vernon Dahmer was killed in Mississippi by a fire bomb on January 10, 1966.

Racist attacks against individuals prevailed throughout the entire Civil Rights Movement. The attacks specifically mentioned here and other racial assaults served to create and maintain an atmosphere of intimidation for all who would challenge existing racist practices.

The Civil Rights Movement was occasioned also by widespread rioting within black communities. Rioting by blacks spread throughout the United States during the 1960's and was probably most prevalent during the years 1964 through 1968. Numerous riots in many American cities resulted in deaths, injuries, arrests and extensive property damage. A major riot occurred, for example, in August of 1965 in Watts, a suburb of Los Angeles. The Watts' riot, which was precipitated by the arrest of a young black man, continued for a period of five days and resulted in 34 deaths, more than one thousand injuries, and 4,000 arrests. The estimated property damage was $40 million.

Riots broke out in 1968 in 125 American cities following the assassination of civil rights leader Dr. Martin Luther King, Jr. The 1968 riots resulted in approximately 46 deaths, 3,500 injuries, 20,000 arrests, and more than $45 million in property damage.

As a result of the Civil Rights Movement, the practice of forced racial segregation was abandoned. Federal and state laws were enacted prohibiting many racially discriminatory practices. We adopted a national policy of equal opportunity for all. We implemented state and federal programs of affirmative action to help uplift blacks in education, employment, business and other aspects of our society. We moved in 1965 to enact the Federal Voting Rights Act that gives important protection to blacks and others in the exercise of the right to vote.

The Civil Rights Movement resulted also in an enhanced sense of pride and dignity among black people. Prior to the 1960's, blacks were required in many cases to degrade themselves when merely coming into contact with whites. Humiliation and insult were inherent in the very practice of racial segregation. As a result of racial degradation, being black for some blacks was a bad and unfortunate thing. Being called black was offensive. Some blacks made efforts even to deny their skin color. Some tried to adapt their physical appearance, with hair styles, skin bleaching and the like, so as to imitate the appearance of whites.

During the 1960's, blacks began to take pride in their own physical appearance. They developed pride in their hair and in the color of their skin. They also looked back to their history for a sense of heritage. They became proud of their African ancestry. Blacks developed a whole new outlook about themselves, an outlook that was reflected, and in fact still is reflected, in the manner in which they talk and dress and go about their affairs in general.

Some Americans have reached the conclusion, on the basis of the improvement in our race relations, as a result of the Civil Rights Movement, that the racial problem in the United States has now been resolved, and that there is nothing further to be done with respect to racial equality. Some Americans are of the opinion that no further legitimate complaints can be made regarding the treatment of blacks.

But racial inequities, racial insults, and racial hatred are still with us. And while many Americans may be willing to accept our current situation as it is, the black people of our country and many other Americans are not. The racial problem in the United States has not been resolved. And we are not, at least at this point and time, even moving in the direction of an ultimate resolution. Current efforts against racial inequities are inadequate. Some efforts are even misguided and are actually aggravating our racial situation.

The solution to our problem is total and complete racial equality. Blacks will not give up the quest for justice. Blacks will not accept a subordinate position in our society. They never have. And now, more than ever, with an enhanced sense of pride and self respect, they never will.

Determination among blacks to achieve racial equality is precisely what a nation such as ours would expect. That human spirit that moves Americans in general to seek freedom and justice, and induces Americans to make enormous sacrifices, including the giving of their lives, in defense of basic freedoms and for other righteous causes, is the same spirit that motivates blacks in their quest for true equality of treatment.

Equality of treatment is not something that blacks today merely desire. Rather, it is a basic human right to which they feel most emphatically entitled. They also feel equality of treatment is attainable. The accomplishments of some blacks, and current laws and policies, that expound principles of equal opportunity for all, have created very definite expectations about equality.

The struggle against racial inequities will continue for as long as racial inequities are with us. The absence today of protest activities like those of the Civil Rights Movement should not be interpreted at all as an indication that black protest is over. There have been ups and downs and adjustments and readjustments, throughout our history, in the fight for racial equality. There have been periods of turmoil and periods of relative calm. National and world affairs, the emergence of certain personalities, changes in the issues presented, and other factors greatly influence the nature and character of anti-racist activities. Relative calm, here and there, does not mean all is well.

There can be no question that improved race relations did contribute in ending the racial turmoil of the Civil Rights Movement. But improved race relations was not the only factor. The sit-in campaigns and the public demonstrations of the 1950's and 1960's were involved primarily with efforts to change racist laws and racist practices. Sit-in campaigns and public demonstrations were involved with specific issues such as forced segregation, the right to vote, and racial discrimination sanctioned or permitted by law. We now have laws prohibiting many racist practices. Consequently, it would be pointless today, even though racial injustice still exists, to demand laws against racist practices. Equal opportunity for all is already the stated law of the land.

Racial discrimination today is very insidious. It is difficult in many instances, if not altogether impossible, to distinguish and isolate offending racial conduct. Protest activities like those of the Civil Rights Movement are not well suited for today's racial issues, as those issues are currently defined.

Blacks have now turned, at least temporarily, to methods other than public protest to eliminate racial inequities. But, as indicated, current methods are not resolving our problems. Blacks will soon be forced to redefine the issues, and to look to other avenues for equality, perhaps again, when suitable issues or objects are identified, to public demonstrations and other activities of confrontation.

The possibility of widespread protest is not the only problem presented by our racial situation. Our racial situation is serving also to promote and maintain deep feelings of racial animosity. Many Americans are strongly motivated by racial suspicion, racial hatred and racial resentment. These underlying racial hostilities can be ignited into explosive racial confrontations.

Consider, for example, the December, 1986 incident in New York City, Queens borough, involving a racist attack on three black men by a gang of whites. One of the victims of that attack was chased into the path of a passing motor vehicle and was struck and killed. In a subsequent separate incident in another neighborhood, a white teenager, not involved in the initial occurrence, was beaten by black youths apparently in retaliation. Black youths chanted, "Kill the whites the way they kill us."[4]

As a result of the attack on the three black men, racial tensions among blacks and whites were intensified. Fortunately, racial hostilities did not result, in this particular situation, in a series of acts of racial violence. We cannot expect, however, to continue to be so lucky. Feelings today of hatred and resentment can lead to explosive racial confrontations and widespread violence, with extensive property damage, and senseless injuries and deaths.

There is danger in our racial situation also in that current efforts against racial inequities are leaving blacks frustrated and angry. There is frustration and anger in that racial inequities are not being eliminated. There is frustration and anger in that blacks must contend with racial insults and other racially derogatory treatment. There is frustration and anger in that equal opportunity is still not a reality.

Frustration and anger can result in violence. Riots in particular arise out of these emotions. In fact, for most riots of the Civil Rights Movement, there is no other plausible explanation. Most riots of the Civil Rights Movement were spontaneous in nature and without specific aims to improve the condition of blacks. Most riots of the Civil Rights Movement were actually self destructive in that they led to deaths, injuries and extensive property damage within black communities. The riots of the Civil Rights Movement occurred in general, not as measures by blacks to uplift blacks, but out of anger and frustration.

The racial situation in the United States is a problem. Blacks are continuing to struggle for equality of treatment. Racial tensions among blacks and whites are increasing. Anger and frustration are intensifying. Protest activities, racist attacks against individuals, rioting and/or other racial occurrences will develop, in time, so as to thoroughly arouse existing hostilities and frustrations, and take us into yet another era of racial turmoil, of the magnitude perhaps (or even greater) of the turmoil of the Civil Rights Movement of the 1950's and 1960's.

Significant racial turmoil would result in the loss of lives, personal injuries, frustrations, property damage, inconveniences, and anxieties. Expenses would be incurred in efforts to restore and maintain order. Time and energy would be expended in attending to the problems. There would be other detriments as well, tangible and intangible, to individuals and our nation.

We certainly made it through the turmoil of the Civil Rights Movement without catastrophic consequences to our nation, and without acts of violence ever physically reaching the neighborhoods of most American citizens. One ought not to conclude, however, on the basis of our past experience, that racial turmoil today would be containable.

Necessary measures, such as police presence, arrests, criminal prosecutions and the like, against blacks engaged in riots and other violent activities, would result in concerns and anxieties among blacks in general. Some police activities would probably be regarded by blacks as racially offensive. Deaths in confrontation with the police truly would not be well received. Young black boys, even though misguided, dying on the streets of America for a decent and dignified way of life would arouse the black community.

The white people of our country would also be moved, but many by an altogether different sentimentality. The violent activities of some blacks would result in a backlash against blacks in general. Whites would be angered and outraged by any violence that threatened them in their persons, possessions, convenience or sensibilities.

Intolerance and indignation would prevail in American attitudes and American behavior. Increased racial hostilities would result in an increase in racial assaults and other racially discriminatory practices. Racial turmoil has the capacity, as it develops, to reach out and engage many many Americans not initially involved.

And racial turmoil, even if physically confined, would still be unacceptable to the American people. Racial turmoil would be an irrefutable attestation that there are indeed racial problems in the United States. And, as such, it would be a challenge as to whether we are truly committed, as we say we are, to the fundamental American values of fairness and equal opportunity for all. This challenge would have to be answered.

Additionally, racial turmoil is unacceptable for some solely because it is unsightly. Some people feel racial turmoil is offensive and repulsive, and has no place in a society as great and beautiful as ours.

Racial turmoil, even if physically confined, would mobilize our country to attend to the situation presented. Racial issues would be considered and debated in newspapers and magazines, on radio and television, in state and federal legislative sessions, in federal and state executive action, in political elections as candidates take certain positions, in conversations at our jobs and in our homes, and in general in the lives our citizens. Our racial situation would become a dominate issue in our everyday lives.

Some Americans would insist on a law and order approach to the problem, and would demand a severe police crackdown on all who participate in undesirable activities. Others would urge that we concentrate on eliminating underlying inequities. Debate on how to respond to our situation and other issues of controversy would serve to divide the American people.

Racial turmoil's initial disturbance of the peace would not be the principal problem. The true danger in racial turmoil is that we would become politically and emotionally preoccupied with the issues and the situation, and thus would not be in a position to give our best effort in attending to other matters affecting our lives. We would become focused on our racial situation to the detriment of other important considerations. What should be of special concern in this regard is the national security of the United States.

We live in a world that continues each day to grow more and more volatile. Activities outside our borders are of great concern to us. It is important that world affairs not develop in a way to threaten our nation. It is important that political, social and military occurrences in certain regions of the world not be controlled by foreign powers with interests that conflict with our own.

Our ability to influence foreign developments is crucial to the security of the United States. Of course, other powers seek to influence certain developments in their self interest as well. Competition for influence in world affairs is such that we cannot afford to become preoccupied in dealing with domestic disquietude. Not only would our attention be diverted from external threats, but racial conflict would divide us and thus impair us politically in our ability to manage matters of foreign relations.

Our ability to conduct matters of foreign policy in our own best interest would be impaired in another respect as well. The foreign policy of the United States depends, at least in part, on world public opinion. When we seek to influence other countries, particularly with respect to human rights, we may be asked to first set our own house in order. The affairs of blacks in Africa and the affairs of minorities throughout the world are issues of great importance. If we are to have influence with regard to these issues we must be credible. And we cannot be credible with racial turmoil or deteriorated race relations within our own borders.

The notion that our racial situation is a problem for black people only is grossly misguided. Our racial situation is a problem for all of us. It is a problem potentially even in matters of national security. It is a problem not given the attention it requires. We are a considerate people with great intellect and imagination and yet, insofar as the consequences of our race relations are concerned, we have shown an unfortunate lack of foresight. It should be apparent to anyone who thinks about our situation that something frightening and very dangerous is happening to us.

CHAPTER 2

RACIAL INEQUITIES

The fact that racial inequities result in violence and other detriments is certainly not proof that racial inequities actually exist. Indeed, we go about our affairs essentially as if they do not exist. And why shouldn't we? After all, racial discrimination in the United States is prohibited by state and federal laws. Our national public policy is equal opportunity for all our citizens. Moreover, and most important of all, Americans are decent fair minded people who just do not make it their business to violate the legitimate human rights of others.

Of course, we must concede that we do have certain racially segregated neighborhoods. And, in general, we must acknowledge the truth that blacks as a group do not do as well as whites in our country. We are aware of the bad economic and poor housing conditions of blacks. But, as a nation, we do not accept the proposition that the problems blacks face today are being caused by racial injustice. The view that past racial injustice contributes to the current condition of blacks is also widely rejected. And among many who feel past wrongs do contribute to current black problems, there is a feeling that it would be unfair to implement remedies that call upon whites today to make sacrifices.

As a nation, we behave as though we have a good and clear conscience in all things regarding matters of race. A good and clear conscience, however, does not preclude racial discord. Racial conflict will continue whether or not we personally believe we have been righteous. Racial conflict will continue for as long as blacks persist with the struggle for equality of treatment. And blacks will continue with that struggle for as long as their position in our society is subordinate to that of whites.

The current struggle for racial equality is deeply rooted in the belief that racial inequities are indeed the result of wrongs committed against blacks. Of course, the fact alone that blacks do not do as well as whites does not constitute a wrong. And one must not be misled by the mere allegation of racism, or by the controversial or highly emotional nature of race-related issues. The essential question presented is whether, as a matter of conscience or some other consideration, there are in fact racial inequities for which we should be held accountable.

It is important, in considering the essential question presented, to inquire as to all detriments to blacks on the basis of skin color, whether the result of past or present activity, legal or illegal behavior, or malicious or non malicious conduct. It would be a mistake, in examining our racial situation, to restrict ourselves, for example, to the question of whether American citizens are racists, or whether they are conforming their conduct to the requirements of the law. An approach restricted in such a manner simply would not address the total and complete problem presented.

Race-Consciousness

The basic and fundamental detriment to blacks today is race-consciousness. Although racial discrimination is prohibited by law in many aspects of our society, we currently have no programs or policies against the practice or promotion of race-consciousness. To the contrary, race-consciousness in the United States is vigorously encouraged and reinforced. On television, on the radio, in newspapers, in magazines and in our daily conversations, we speak of "the black man," "the black woman," "the black youth," "the black lawyer," "the black doctor," "the black vote," "the black mayor," "the black astronaut," and the like. Race is tremendously important to us. And our persistent recognition of blacks as black does not just mean blacks have black skin. There are in fact certain implications, innuendoes, condescensions and subtleties inherent in the very practice of race-consciousness that represent and convey the opinion, not only that blacks are different, but that they are different in a negative rather than in a neutral or favorable way.

Race-consciousness, as practiced in the United States, is an insult and a degradation to our black citizens. And this indignity to blacks is not, by any means, inconsequential. Racial indignity is quite painful and very very real, and has a tremendous adverse effect on the quality of life for black people. Racial indignity itself is a grievous and deplorable wrong that truly ought to be recognized and regarded as such. After all, we all want and expect to be treated in our lives with a certain level of human dignity. Indeed, many of us regard human dignity as a fundamental right for which we are prepared to die.

Additionally, race-consciousness causes racial discrimination. Of course, theoretically, negative attitudes about blacks need not result in discrimination. As a practical matter, however, it would be quite naive to actually believe racial attitudes do not affect us in our behavior. And the harm to blacks is not altogether precluded by existing civil rights legislation. In many situations, especially those involving individuals with comparable skills and qualifications, decisions as to who, among the qualified, are best qualified for various considerations are matters of personal judgment, arising basically out of personal impressions and perceptions. Thus, great personal discretion, essentially beyond the reach of laws against discrimination, plays a pervasive and dominate role in the ultimate award of jobs, promotions, and other important benefits in our society. And we are greatly influenced in our personal discretion, whether with or without racist intent, by the racial attitudes maintained and promoted by race-consciousness.

Race-consciousness induces individuals also not to develop meaningful work, business, social and personal relationships with others of a different color. As a result, blacks are being denied open and free association, and all the benefits, privileges and opportunities derived therefrom. And, as in the case with discrimination, the particular conduct involved is beyond the reach of civil rights legislation.

Personal discretion in association cannot be eliminated in all situations by rules or regulations. And, indeed, no effort in this regard is being made. No such effort should be made. Discretion in association, with exceptions, is a right that must be respected. The exercise of this discretion, however, on a race-conscious basis is a wrong that has no place among people truly committed to human rights.

Race-consciousness creates certain expectations as well that function as a power and force of great intimidation against non discriminatory conduct. People otherwise inclined to develop relationships across racial lines, for example, frequently do not do so for fear that others would shun or disapprove of such behavior. Furthermore, race-consciousness produces an atmosphere very receptive to assaults against blacks. Our dealings with matters of race generate the impression, for far too many people, that the American public has either a desire, indifference, or great tolerance for violence and other wrongs against our black citizens.

The underlying problem in our race relations is race-consciousness itself. And although this truth may seem strange to some, it can be understood. It can be understood by considering the actual course of events in our evolvement as a race-conscious nation. Indeed, consideration of our history may be essential to a true understanding as to the real nature and character of our current race-conscious practices.

Our Evolvement as a Race-Conscious Nation

Our development as a race-conscious people was greatly influenced in the beginning by the participation of European attitudes and practices in our affairs. In 1869, an Alabama state judge described that participation as follows, ". . . it is a fact fully established by public history, that at the time when these colonies were planted, negro slavery and the slave trade were not only recognized as lawful, but sanctioned and protected by all the enlightened commercial nations of Europe. England, France, Spain and Portugal were rivals in every market, in which a profit was to be realized from the trade, and the right to buy and sell negro slaves was everywhere admitted. . . . Negro slavery was thus introduced into the colonies through the mother country, and with the consent of the colonists."[1]

England began establishing colonies along the east coast of North America in the seventeenth century. Black and white indentured servants were used to clear forests and cultivate fields. The supply of servants proved to be inadequate to meet the great demand for labor and the colonies began to rely on the importation of black slaves from Africa. The slave trade flourished. Southern colonies became especially dependent on slaves to produce crops on plantations.

The American colonies declared their independence from England in 1776. The Constitution of the United States was approved by convention delegates on September 17, 1787. Our country was born. But, unfortunately, like a newborn baby addicted to the drug heroin, it was born thoroughly and completely addicted to slavery and also to race-consciousness. And after birth, the situation worsened. The 1793 invention of the cotton gin by Eli Whitney made it possible for Southern plantations to export a greatly increased volume of cotton. Slaves were used to run cotton gins and to cultivate and harvest cotton crops.

Race-consciousness Prior To Emancipation

Slavery persisted throughout the Colonial era of America and thereafter in the United States for a total period of more than two hundred years. During this period, slaves were defined by law as property, and thus had no legal, political or human rights. The legal status of slaves in 1828 was described by a state Judge in a court case as follows, "I further maintain that, in this country, a slave is in absolute bondage; that he has no civil right and can hold no property except at the will and pleasure of his master; that his master is his guardian and protector, and that all his rights, acquisitions, and services are in the hands of his master; . . . and that whatever he lawfully acquires and gains is the acquirement and possession of the master."[2]

Slavery and racist attitudes in America resulted in the enactment of certain laws that regulated not only the conduct of blacks, both slave and free, but also the conduct of others toward blacks. Although each jurisdiction had its own set of rules, race laws throughout the country, especially those in slave states, were very similar in their requirements. Blacks could not be taught to read or write and were restricted as to where they could reside. Blacks could not be disrespectful or use insolent or abusive language to whites. They were prohibited by law from insulting whites and were not allowed to conceive of themselves as being "equal." Violations of some codes of behavior resulted in harsh punishment such as beatings and cropping of the ears.[3]

Violence against blacks was commonplace. Masters in particular had great discretion in the use of violence against their slaves. Consider, for example, the 1839 North Carolina case of State v Hoover that involved the criminal prosecution of a master who brutally beat and killed his female slave. The female slave in this case was beaten while she was pregnant. She was beaten also immediately after she gave birth. Five wounds were inflicted to her head a week before she died. A subsequent wound to the head was determined to be the cause of death.

In delivering the decision of the court in the case, Judge Ruffin wrote, "A master may lawfully punish his slave; and the degree must, in general, be left to his own judgment and humanity, and can not be judicially questioned. . . . But the master's authority is not altogether unlimited. He must not kill. There is, at least, this restriction upon his power: he must stop short of taking life. . . . If death unhappily ensue from the master's chastisement of his slave, inflicted apparently with a good intent, for reformation or example, and with no purpose to take life or to put it in jeopardy, the law would doubtless tenderly regard every circumstance which, judging from the conduct generally of masters towards slaves, might reasonably be supposed to have hurried the party into excess."[4]

The master charged in the case was convicted of murder. And the conviction was allowed to stand, but apparently only because the brutality against the slave was not intended to correct, chastise, or maintain discipline.

Strong courageous efforts were made prior to the Civil War to abolish slavery in the United States. But slavery, certainly cruel and despicable, was merely one aspect of the total race problem. The truth of this assertion is found not only in the race laws that existed in various states prior to Emancipation,[5] but also and especially in the Dred Scott case that was decided in 1856 by the United States Supreme Court.[6]

Dred Scott was a slave who sought emancipation for himself, his wife and his two daughters. Freedom was claimed on the basis of their prior residence in the Upper Louisiana Territory where slavery was prohibited by Congress. Dred Scott himself had also resided prior to marriage in the non slave state of Illinois. The Dred Scott law suit, which was originally filed in the Circuit Court of the United States for the District of Missouri, presented questions of enormous importance for consideration by the Court. The dominant question was whether blacks were citizens of the

United States entitled to the rights, privileges and immunities guaranteed by the United States Constitution.

The Supreme Court was required to interpret Section Two of the Fourth Article of the Constitution. The pertinent part of that section provides, "The Citizens of each State shall be entitled to all Privileges and Immunities of Citizens in the several States." An interpretation declaring blacks citizens would have extended to blacks the full protection of the Fourth Article and protection also of other Constitutional provisions. Many state laws that placed restrictions on blacks would have been invalidated.

Chief Justice Taney, who delivered the opinion of the Court in the case, was very much aware of the consequences of a ruling in favor of Dred Scott. Mr. Justice Taney wrote, "And if persons of the African race are citizens of a State, and of the United States, they would be entitled to all these privileges and immunities in every State, and the State could not restrict them; for they would hold these privileges and immunities under paramount authority of the Federal Government, and its courts would be bound to maintain and enforce them, the Constitution and the laws of the State to the contrary, notwithstanding. And if the States could limit or restrict them, or place the party in an inferior grade, this clause of the Constitution would be unmeaning, and could have no operation; and would give no rights to the citizen when in another State."[7] Thus, citizenship rights for blacks presented two alternatives both very unattractive to the Chief Justice: the elimination of many race-conscious state laws and practices or a deadly blow to the integrity of the Fourth Article of the Constitution.

The Supreme Court ruled in the case that persons of African descent were not citizens of the United States. The Court expressed the view that blacks could become state citizens if allowed by state laws, but that state citizenship would not confer citizenship rights under the Constitution of the United States.

The Supreme Court determined that the framers of the Constitution of the United States did not intend to include blacks as citizens. As evidence of the framers' intent, the Court referred to the state of public opinion regarding blacks at the time the Constitution was adopted. The Chief Justice described that state of public opinion as follows: "They had for more than a century before been regarded as beings of an inferior order, and altogether unfit to associate with the white race, either in social or political relations; and so far inferior, that they had no rights which the white man was bound to respect; and that the Negro might justly and lawfully be reduced to slavery for his benefit."[8] It was perfectly understood, in Mr. Justice Taney's view, that the Constitution did not intend to embrace blacks as citizens.

Chief Justice Taney expressed opinions also as to the other issues involved in the case. The Justice concluded that the Scott family was not entitled to emancipation on the basis of their residence in the Upper Louisiana Territory. The Act of Congress prohibiting slavery in that territory was unconstitutional, in the Chief Justice's view, and therefore void and of no consequence. As to Dred Scott's prior residence in the State of Illinois, Mr. Justice Taney stated that the law of Missouri was controlling. Thus, Dred Scott's legal status was determined by the slave laws of Missouri and not by the laws of Illinois where slavery was prohibited.

Racial Discrimination Following The Civil War

The rulings in the Dred Scott case placed the Constitution of the United States squarely in the path of efforts to improve the conditions of blacks. Thus, it was necessary, after the Civil War, to enact Constitutional Amendments. The Constitution had to be changed to prohibit slavery rather than to protect it. It was necessary also to confer citizenship rights on blacks and to restrict states in their power to deny opportunities to citizens on the basis of skin color.

Three Amendments to the Constitution were ratified during the years immediately following the Civil War: the Thirteenth Amendment on December 18, 1865, the Fourteenth Amendment on July 28, 1868 and the Fifteenth Amendment on March 30, 1870. The Thirteenth Amendment prohibits slavery within the United States. The Fourteenth Amendment gives citizenship rights to all persons born or naturalized in the United States and prohibits States from denying citizens equal protection of the laws. The Fourteenth Amendment provides also that States shall not deprive persons of life, liberty or property without due process, or abridge the privileges or immunities of our citizens. The Fifteenth Amendment states, "The right of citizens of the United States to vote shall not be denied or abridged by the United States or by any State on account of race, color, or previous condition of servitude." The Fifteenth Amendment gives Congress the power to enact legislation to enforce its provisions.

In addition to the Constitutional Amendments, the Congress of the United States moved to enact civil rights legislation. In 1875 the Congress enacted a Civil Rights Act which provided for full and equal enjoyment of public accommodations by all citizens without regard to race or color. Individuals denied rights or privileges guaranteed by the Act were allowed to recover penalties from offenders. Offenders were also subject to criminal prosecution.

The authority of Congress to enact the Civil Rights Act of 1875 was challenged in the United States Supreme Court in 1883. Five individual cases were considered.[9] Two of the five cases involved criminal charges against individuals for denying blacks accommodations and privileges in an inn or motel. Two cases involved criminal charges against individuals for denying blacks privileges and accommodations of a theater. The other case involved a claim for damages for a conductor's refusal to allow a black woman to ride in a railroad car.

The Supreme Court stated the authority of Congress, if any, to enact the Civil Rights Act of 1875 had to be found in the post Civil War Amendments. No one would contend, the court observed, that such authority existed prior to the Amendments.

The Court inquired, after noting that the Fourteenth Amendment prohibited State action only, whether the legislation of 1875 actually addressed state action. The court answered, "An inspection of the law shows that it makes no reference whatever to any supposed or apprehended violation of the Fourteenth Amendment on the part of States. It is not predicated on any such view. It proceeds ex directo to declare that certain acts committed by individuals shall be deemed offences, and shall be prosecuted and punished by proceedings in the courts of the United States. It does not profess to be corrective of any constitutional wrong committed by the States; it does not make its operation to depend upon any such wrong committed."[10] The Court ruled that the legislative provisions in question were not authorized by the Fourteenth Amendment.

The Court concluded also that Congress did not have the authority pursuant to the Thirteenth Amendment to enact the legislation. The Court was of the opinion that the Thirteenth Amendment gave Congress the power to regulate the activities of individuals as to slavery only. The denial of privileges and accommodations in inns, public conveyances and the like were not deemed to constitute slavery. The Congressional effort of 1875 to provide for equal enjoyment of public accommodations was declared unconstitutional.

The Congress of the United States was without authority also to protect blacks in situations of employment. The Constitutional restrictions on Congress in this regard were articulated in the 1905 case of Hodges v United States.[11] This case involved whites who used weapons to force blacks off their jobs. The white perpetrators were convicted under federal statute and the convictions were appealed to the United States Supreme Court. The Court was asked to overturn the convictions and declare the statutory provisions involved in the case unconstitutional and void.

Section 1977 of the federal criminal statute provided, "All persons within the jurisdiction of the United States shall have the same right in every state and territory to make and enforce contracts, to sue, be parties, give evidence, and to the full and equal benefit of all laws and proceedings for the security of persons and property as is enjoyed by white citizens, and shall be subject to like punishment, pains, penalties, taxes, licenses and exaction of every kind, and no other." Section 5508 of the statute provided, "If two or more persons conspire to injure, oppress, threaten, or intimidate any citizen in the free exercise or enjoyment of any right or privilege secured him by the Constitution or laws of the United States, or because of his having so exercised the same; . . . shall be fined not more than five thousand dollars and imprisoned no more than ten years;. . ."

Mr. Justice Brewer, who delivered the opinion of the Supreme Court in the case, stated there was no need to look beyond the Thirteenth Amendment for Congressional authority to enact the legislation upon which the convictions were based. The Justice noted that the Fourteenth and Fifteenth Amendments prohibited state action only and clearly did not apply to the activities of individuals.

Mr. Justice Brewer observed that the Thirteenth Amendment prohibited slavery and involuntary servitude. The Thirteenth Amendment did not, in the opinion of the Court, prohibit other racial injustices. The federal government argued, in support of the convictions, that the statute in question did indeed pertain to servitude in that the intimidation used to prevent blacks from performing their contracts was an incident of slavery.

The government's argument was rejected by the Court. The attack on the black workers was not deemed to be slavery. The Court ruled that the federal statutory provisions at issue in the case were unconstitutional. The criminal convictions against the perpetrators were not allowed to stand.

Blacks were without protection as well in the exercise of the right to vote. The right to vote was denied, notwithstanding the provisions of the Fifteenth Amendment.

For many years following the Civil War, political candidates in Southern states needed only to obtain the Democratic Party's nomination to be elected to office. Attitudes and political realities were such that the great majority of all qualified voters cast their votes consistently for Democratic Party candidates. Candidates from other political parties just did not win. As a practical matter, candidates for public office were being elected, not in general elections, which were always won by Democrats, but in Democratic Party primary elections in which blacks were not allowed to participate. The right of blacks to vote in general elections was essentially of no consequence.

In the 1924 case of Nixon v Herndon, a Texas law that provided for white only Democratic Party primary elections was found by the Supreme Court to be offensive to the Constitution.[12] This case did not, however, put an end to the white only primary practice. The exclusion of blacks continued thereafter, not by state action, but by the acts of private individuals. The Supreme Court refused in 1935 in the Grovey v Townsend case to invalidate a white only resolution adopted by the Democratic Convention of Texas.[13] The resolution in question provided, "Be it resolved, that all white citizens of the State of Texas who are qualified to vote under the Constitution and laws of the state shall be eligible to membership in the Democratic party and as such entitled to participate in its deliberations." It was the Supreme Court's view that the resolution adopted by the Democratic Convention was permissible in that it was the action of a private organization, and was not implemented or maintained by the state. State action excluding blacks would have been prohibited by the Fourteenth and Fifteenth Amendments.

In the 1944 case of Smith v Allwright, the Supreme Court changed its attitude regarding the white only primary. In its written opinion of the case, the Court stated, "Primary elections are conducted by the party under the state statutory authority. The county executive committee selects precinct election officials and the county, district or state executive committees, respectively, canvass the returns. . . . We think that this statutory system for the selection of party nominees for inclusion on the general election ballot makes the party which is required to follow these legislative directions an agency of the State in so far as it determines the participants in a primary election."[14] The Court concluded, with regard to the particular facts of the case, that the exclusion of blacks from primary elections by a political party constituted state action in violation of the Constitution of the United States.

The demise of the white only primary did not end the racist denial of voting rights. Violence, intimidation and other practices continued to keep blacks away from the polls. Relief was not obtained from many oppressive practices until the enactment in 1965 of the federal Voting Rights Act.

Literacy tests were also used to disenfranchise the black population. Voters were required by law, for example, to read and interpret state constitutions to the satisfaction of voter registration authorities. Literacy requirements were embodied with such wide discretion that decisions as to who would be allowed to vote were left essentially to the personal judgment of state officials. State officials, of course, were compelled by existing racist practices to determine, without regard to actual literacy performance, that whites satisfied literacy requirements and that blacks did not.[15]

Residence requirements, property qualifications and poll taxes were used also to deny blacks the right to vote. Many requirements threatened the voting rights of a great number of whites as well. The clear and unmistakable purpose and indeed the actual effect of the voting requirements, however, was the disenfranchisement of black citizens.

The civil rights legislation enacted by the Congress following the Civil

War was certainly a strong effort to eliminate harmful distinctions based on race. One can only speculate as to what our current situation would be if that legislation had been allowed to stand. The Supreme Court of the United States was compelled by the Constitution, however, the very document that guarantees individual rights and freedoms, to turn back Congressional attempts to protect the rights and freedoms of blacks. Protection of the privileges and immunities of citizens from attacks by individuals was reserved exclusively for the states. But the states did not protect the rights of blacks. Consequently, with the exception of slavery, the racist customs and practices of individuals that existed prior to the Civil War were allowed to continue. Intimidation and violence were used to deny rights, opportunities and privileges to our black citizens. Racial insult and racial degradation dominated personal, business and social relationships. The post Civil War civil rights Amendments to the Constitution, although grand in their declarations, were essentially ineffective in eliminating racist practices.

The Separate But Equal Doctrine

The single most disturbing blow to civil rights efforts following the Civil War was dealt by the Supreme Court in 1896 in the case of Plessy v Ferguson.[16] This case involved a Louisiana state law that required railway companies carrying passengers to provide equal but separate accommodations for white and colored races. Railway companies were required to partition passenger coaches or provide more than one coach for each passenger train. Persons were prohibited from taking seats in coaches or compartments other than those reserved for the race to which they belonged. Officers of railway companies were required to assign passengers to seats according to their race. Those who refused to abide by the requirements of the law were subject to fines or imprisonment.

Plessy challenged the Louisiana law in state court and lost. He then took the matter to the Supreme Court of the United States. The Supreme Court affirmed the state court's judgment and ruled that the law in question did not violate either the Thirteenth or Fourteenth Amendment to the Constitution.

The written opinion of the Court in the case, which was delivered by Mr. Justice Brown, represented the views of all the Supreme Court Justices except Justices Brewer and Harlan. Mr. Justice Brewer did not participate in the case. Mr. Justice Harlan wrote a separate opinion in disagreement with the Court's ruling.

Mr. Justice Brown did not believe Plessy was strenuously relying on the argument that the Louisiana law requiring segregation violated the Thirteenth Amendment's prohibition against slavery and involuntary servitude. Mr. Justice Brown maintained that the Thirteenth Amendment abolished slavery as it had existed previously in the United States. It abolished the state of bondage and the practice of people owning other people. The Thirteenth Amendment was not deemed to prohibit all distinctions based on race or all acts of racial discrimination. The Louisiana law did not, in Mr. Justice Brown's opinion, tend to "reestablish a state of involuntary servitude."

The Fourteenth Amendment's guarantee of citizenship rights and equal protection of the laws was also not meant, in Mr. Justice Brown's opinion, to abolish distinctions based on race. Mr. Justice Brown believed the nature of things was such that the abolition of racial distinctions could not have been intended. The view that racial segregation precluded equality of treatment was rejected. The point was made that forced segregation had been previously practiced in states where the rights of blacks had been long and "most earnestly enforced." The observation was made that separate schools for blacks and whites had been allowed in Massachusetts, the District of Columbia and other states. The observation was made that laws forbidding the intermarriage of blacks and whites had also been upheld.

It was argued in the case on behalf of Plessy that if forced segregation could be justified, then there would be justification also for separating people on the basis of hair color. It was suggested that states would be able to prohibit blacks and whites from walking on the same side of the streets or from having their houses painted the same color. Mr. Justice Brown's response to this argument was that, "every exercise of police power must be reasonable, and extend only to such laws as are enacted in good faith for the promotion of the public good, and not for the annoyance or oppression of a particular class."[17]

Apparently, the Supreme Court's majority did not believe Louisiana intended to oppress black citizens. The Court was not persuaded, it appears, that segregation was capable of doing harm. The Court embraced the view that segregation did not tend "to destroy the legal equality of the two races." Any badge of inferiority incident to forced segregation was, in the Court's view, the fault not of segregation but of blacks who perceived themselves as being inferior.

The Court's majority held the view also that racial prejudices could not be overcome by legislation or by "enforced commingling of the two races." With regard to this issue, Mr. Justice Brown wrote, "Legislation is powerless to eradicate racial instincts or abolish distinctions based upon physical differences, and the attempt to do so can only result in accentuating the difficulties of the present situation. If the civil and political rights of both races be equal one cannot be inferior to the other civilly or politically. If one race be inferior to the other socially, the Constitution of the United States cannot put them upon the same plane."[18] But Plessy was not seeking forced integration by legislation or by constitutional doctrine. He was simply requesting that states not be allowed to impose racial segregation on their citizens by state law.

Mr. Justice Harlan's dissent strongly disputed the majority's interpretation of the Thirteenth and Fourteenth Amendments. Mr. Justice Harlan believed the Thirteenth Amendment protected all rights necessarily inherent in freedom. He believed the Thirteenth Amendment prohibited the "imposition of any burdens or disabilities that constitute badges of slavery and servitude." Mr. Justice Harlan took the position that the Louisiana law before the court was in direct conflict with the prohibition against slavery.

Mr. Justice Harlan was not at all impressed, as was the Court's majority, by previous state court decisions allowing segregation. With regard to those decisions, Mr. Justice Harlan wrote, "Some, and the most important, of them, are wholly inapplicable, because rendered prior to the adoption of the last amendments to the constitution, when colored people had very few rights which the dominant race felt obliged to respect. Others were made at a time when public opinion, in many localities, was dominated by the institution of slavery; when it would not have been safe to do justice to the black man; and when, so far as the rights of blacks were concerned, race prejudice was, practically, the supreme law of the land. Those decisions cannot be guides in the era introduced by recent amendments of the supreme law, which established universal civil freedom, gave citizenship to all born or naturalized in the United States, and residing here, obliterated the race line from our systems of governments, national and state, and placed our free institutions upon the broad and sure foundation of the equality of all men before the law."[19] It was Mr. Justice Harlan's view that legislation affecting civil rights could not have regard to matters of race.

Mr. Justice Harlan noted that forced segregation deprived both blacks and whites of personal liberty: blacks and whites were prevented by the Louisiana law, without regard to their personal desires, from riding together on passenger trains. Mr. Justice Harlan maintained, "If a white man and a black man choose to occupy the same public conveyance on a public highway, it is their right to do so; and no government, proceeding alone on the grounds of race, can prevent it without infringing on the personal liberty of each. It is one thing for railroad carriers to furnish, or to be required by law to furnish, equal accommodations for all who they are under a legal duty to carry. It is quite another thing for government to forbid citizens of the white and black races from traveling in the same public conveyance, and to punish officers of the railroad companies for permitting persons of the two races to occupy the same passenger coach."[20] Mr. Justice Harlan was convinced that the intent of the Louisiana law was to exclude blacks from coaches reserved for whites. He felt the Court's judgment upholding the law would encourage the belief that the Civil Rights Amendments could be defeated by state legislation.

Mr. Justice Harlan predicted that the majority's ruling in the case would prove to be as "pernicious" as the prior decision in the Dred Scott case that declared blacks were not American citizens. He believed forced segregation was inconsistent with existing boastful claims that freedom existed in the United States. He warned that forced segregation would stimulate aggression against blacks, encourage hate and distrust, and assure continuous racial conflict to the detriment of all American citizens. Mr. Justice Harlan did not wish to give the seed of hate the sanction of law.

States were permitted by the ruling in the Plessy v Ferguson case to compel racial segregation in practically every aspect of American life. Forced racial segregation continued following the decision in the case as a dominant and pervasive practice for a period of more than fifty years. It persisted with the approval and sanction of the Constitution of the United States until well into the 1950's.

In the year 1950, racial segregation in public schools was either required or permitted in twenty-one states and also in the Nation's capitol. Thirty states had laws prohibiting marriage between blacks and whites. Segregation was required in railroad facilities and on buses. It was required in amusement, in hospitals, in penal institutions and in employment. State laws compelled segregation in dining facilities, on street cars, in waiting rooms, on steamboats, on ferries and on street railways. Segregation was also required by city regulations and ordinances.[21]

Despite the abolition of slavery and the Constitutional guarantee of citizenship rights, we continued as a nation, following the Civil War, to attribute great great importance to matters of race. Mr. Justice Harlan's 1896 observations regarding forced segregation proved to be quite prophetic. His concluding comments in the Plessy v Ferguson case on the Louisiana race law contained the following, "If laws of like character should be enacted in the several states of the Union, the effect would be in the highest degree mischievous. Slavery, as an institution tolerated by law, would, it is true, have disappeared from our country; but there would remain a power in the States, by sinister legislation, to interfere with the full enjoyment of the blessings of freedom, to regulate civil rights, common to all citizens, upon the basis of race, and to place in a condition of legal inferiority a large body of American citizens."[22]

Mr. Justice Harlan's fears were quickly realized. The "separate but equal" doctrine evolved into a contradiction within itself. As applied in the various states, the word "equal" did not actually mean equality of privileges, accommodations and opportunities. Separate accommodations and privileges for blacks were rarely equal. Segregation resulted also in many instances in complete denials. Inequality was inherent in the very practice of apartheid. The "separate but equal" doctrine, even when implemented and enforced with good faith, which certainly was not always the case, still resulted in denials to our black citizens.

Consider the good faith application of the "separate but equal" doctrine in the 1943 Maryland case of Durkee v Murphy.[23] The Durkee v Murphy case involved a claim that the golf course for blacks in Baltimore was inferior to other golf courses in the City. In 1943, the City of Baltimore maintained four golf courses in its public parks. Blacks were allowed to use the golf course at Carroll Park only. The other golf courses were reserved for whites.

The City of Baltimore took the position in the case that the Constitution of the United States did not require that blacks be provided with a golf course at all, so long as other facilities at Carroll Park were adequate. The Maryland Court was impressed with the City's position but ruled nevertheless that blacks were indeed entitled to a golf course, a course substantially equal, but not necessarily equal in all respects to golf courses provided for whites. The Court indicated that the City would not be compelled to end the practice of segregation. The Court expressed the view that, if the facilities were found to be unequal, the Board of Park Commissioners of Baltimore could, in its discretion, make the golf course for blacks substantially equal, or admit blacks to "one of the other courses, or to all, as the Board may decide."

The essential harms to blacks in the case were not even addressed by the Maryland Court. Aside from the insult and degradation involved in segregation, black golfers in Baltimore in 1943 were being denied access to three City golf courses that were maintained by taxpayers' money. And no remedy was forthcoming, no matter what, so long as segregation was maintained. The power to segregate was in reality the power to exclude. It was the power to deny and degrade. It was the power to insult. It was the power to force upon blacks inferior privileges and opportunities.

School Segregation

Inequalities in the maintenance of racially segregated schools were especially detrimental to blacks. Consider, for example, the realities of school segregation in Baltimore County in 1937. The white student population in Baltimore County at that time was about ten times greater than the black student population. Some blacks resided in areas throughout the county. Most blacks, however, lived in the thickly populated centers near the city of Baltimore. The black to white student ratio and the settlement of blacks throughout the county made it impractical, if not impossible, for public officials to educate blacks and whites separately and yet under same or similar circumstances.

The school segregation situation in Baltimore County in 1937 was typical. The racial composition and the distribution of blacks in schools districts throughout the country were very similar to the conditions found in Baltimore County. The education of blacks and whites separately and yet under same or similar circumstances was an impractical proposition throughout the United States.

It would have been impractical, for example, for a school district to expend a certain amount of money on a 100,000 volume library for 5,000 white students and expend the same amount for a separate 100,000 volume library for 500 black students. The library for blacks in this example, as a practical matter, would not have consisted of 100,000 volumes. Similarly, it would have been impractical for a school district to expend a certain amount of money on school facilities and teachers for 5,000 white students and provide comparable facilities and teachers for 500 black students. Consistent with existing racial attitudes, the burden of maintaining school segregation was placed whenever possible on black students.

Blacks were often educated in the United States in small numbers and under very unfavorable conditions. Some blacks were forced to travel away from their homes to schools at central locations. These centrally located schools were inferior to white schools in almost every respect: as to teacher to student ratio, subject matters taught, school supplies, school equipment, school buildings and the like. Black students in our country simply did not receive an equal education.

In 1937, Baltimore County provided both elementary schools and high schools for its white students. Schools for blacks were maintained for grades one through seven only. Many of the black elementary schools were small and all subjects and grades were taught by one teacher. For education beyond the seventh grade, blacks were required to attend schools in the City of Baltimore. Baltimore County could not effectively maintain a black high school.

All Baltimore County students, blacks and whites, were required to pass a test before entering high school. Tests were based on the elementary school work of white students. The work of black students was not a consideration in the tests. Also, white students were tested at schools familiar to them while blacks were tested at central locations away from their homes. This testing arrangement obviously placed black students at a decisive disadvantage.

Baltimore County's methods and procedures for providing education were challenged by a black female student in the Maryland case of Williams v Zimmerman.[24] The black student was promoted by her principal from the seventh to the eight grade but failed the County's high school admission test. The County refused on the basis of the test performance to pay the student's tuition to attend the eight grade in the City of Baltimore.

The Court of Appeals of Maryland acknowledged the County's disparate treatment of the races, but refused nevertheless to grant the young black student a remedy. The Court maintained, "Possibly there might be, under some circumstances, inequalities encountered in dealing with the two races separately that would render the maintenance of the separation inconsistent with the constitutional requirement of equal protection of the laws, but the allowance of separate treatment at all involves allowance of some incidental differences, and some inequalities, in meeting practical problems presented. And it is the opinion of the court that the differences here amount to no more."[25]

The Court of Appeals was of the opinion also that admitting the black student to a white school in Baltimore County, which was the remedy sought in the case, would not have resolved all of the problems complained of. With regard to this issue the Court indicated, "Inequalities in the separate elementary school teaching are complained of as having an effect to deny the colored children equal opportunities to qualify for examinations, and thus equal access to the high school course, but this could not be remedied by admitting to a high school a child who is not fitted for it. The remedy would have to be one reaching farther back."[26] The only effective remedy, of course, would have been the complete integration of the Baltimore County school system. It is difficult to believe, however, that the Court of Appeals of Maryland was prepared in 1937 to issue such an order.

Most Americans today would probably agree with Mr. Justice Harlan that the ruling in the Plessy v Ferguson case was a mistake. One can only speculate as to whether the Supreme Court Justices who decided the case truly believed blacks would be provided equal accommodations and privileges under the "separate but equal" doctrine.

Also, one might argue, although indications are to the contrary, that the state legislators of our past who enacted laws requiring segregation sincerely intended to treat blacks and whites the same, and that segregation was not intended as a tool to degrade blacks or to exclude blacks from opportunities afforded to other citizens of the United States. Whether the people who determined our course with regard to racial segregation had good or bad intentions is debatable. The effect of our past practices, however, is very very clear. As a result of forced segregation, blacks were excluded and, as a nation, we were plunged deeper and deeper into the evils of race-consciousness.

The great importance our laws attributed to matters of race was a sad and tragic situation. A horrible limitation was placed on the American people. The laws in the United States created a situation that simply did not permit American citizens to develop without racist ideas and beliefs.

Repudiation of Separate But Equal Doctrine

The Supreme Court of the United States began to indicate an appreciation of the inequities involved in the "separate but equal" doctrine years before forced segregation was actually repudiated. In 1937, at a time certainly when segregation was the law of the land, the Supreme Court ruled in the Missouri Ex Rel. Gaines v Canada case that Missouri's method of providing separate legal education for blacks and whites was in violation of the equal protection clause of the Fourteenth Amendment to the Constitution.[27] Missouri provided legal education for whites within the state, but did not provide a law school for blacks. There was, however, a state procedure for tuition payment for blacks to attend law schools in other states.

The Supreme Court ruled that Missouri's action to provide legal education for whites within the state created a constitutional obligation that legal education be provided within the state also for blacks. Suggestions that out of state black law schools were very advantageous for blacks were, in the Court's opinion, beside the point. The Court rejected the notion that Missouri's constitutional obligation could be satisfied by the state tuition payment procedure.

In 1948 in the case of Sipuel v Board of Regents, the Supreme Court ordered the admission of a black student to the law school at the University of Oklahoma.[28] The law school at that University, which was the only law school maintained by the state, was reserved for white people only. Consistent with its previous decision in the Missouri Ex Rel. Gaines v Canada case, the Court ruled that the state of Oklahoma, in providing legal education for whites, was bound also to provide legal education for blacks.

The Supreme Court's attention was directed in 1950 in the case of Sweatt v Painter to the question of the sufficiency of separate education provided for blacks.[29] The Sweatt v Painter case involved the maintenance of separate law schools for blacks and whites by the state of Texas. The law school at the University of Texas, which refused to admit blacks, had 850 students, sixteen professors, and a library of 65,000 volumes. The separate law school maintained by the state for blacks had only 23 students, five professors, a library of 16,500 volumes and was not fully accredited.

In comparing the two schools the court stated, ". . . we cannot find substantial equality in the educational opportunities offered white and Negro students by the State. In terms of number of the faculty, variety of courses and opportunity for specialization, size of the student body, scope of the library, availability of law review and similar activities, the University of Texas Law School is superior. What is more important, the University of Texas Law School possesses to a far greater degree those qualities which are incapable of objective measurement but which make for greatness in a law school. Such qualities, to name but a few, include reputation of faculty, experience of the administration, position and influence of alumni, standing in the community, traditions and prestige. It is difficult to believe that one who had a free choice between these law schools would consider the question close."[30] The black student petitioner in the case was ordered admitted to the University of Texas Law School.

Also in 1950, the Supreme Court decided the McLaurin v Oklahoma State Regents case that involved the imposition of certain conditions of segregation upon a black student who had been admitted to the previously white only University of Oklahoma.[31] The black student was required pursuant to state law to sit apart from other students in designated places. He was segregated, for example, in classrooms, in the library and in the cafeteria. The Court ruled that the restrictions imposed on the black student denied him equal protection of the laws.

Strict adherence to the Supreme Court's school segregation rulings of 1950 probably would have eliminated segregation in public schools in most school districts throughout the country. Few separately maintained schools for blacks and whites in the United States would have survived the type of scrutiny employed by the Court in the Sweatt v Painter case. The 1950 Supreme Court rulings rendered state compelled school segregation, as a practice approved by the Constitution, although permissible theoretically, essentially and practically an impossibility. Thus, the Supreme Court's ruling in 1954 in the matter entitled Brown v Board of Education, which explicitly declared state compelled school segregation unconstitutional, was but the natural progression of the Court's attitudes and opinions.[32]

The Brown v Board of Education matter actually involved four separate cases, one each from the states of Kansas, South Carolina, Virginia and Delaware.

The Plaintiffs in the Kansas case filed a law suit in the United States District Court for the District of Kansas challenging the segregation of blacks and whites in the elementary schools in Topeka. The Kansas District Court expressed the view that school segregation created a sense of inferiority on the part of blacks that adversely affected their motivation to learn. The District Court believed segregation impeded the mental development of blacks and deprived blacks also of important benefits of racially integrated school systems. The Plaintiffs' request for an injunction prohibiting segregation was nevertheless denied. The Court concluded that the buildings, qualifications of teachers, curricula and transportation in the schools for blacks and whites were substantially equal.

The Plaintiffs in the South Carolina case asked the United States District Court for the Eastern District of South Carolina to prohibit the segregation of whites and blacks in both the elementary schools and high schools in Clarendon County. The District Court made a finding that the schools for blacks in the County were inferior to those for whites. An order was issued requiring that the school facilities be equalized. The Court did not invalidate state laws requiring segregation.

The United States District Court for the Eastern District of Virginia made a finding in the Virginia case that the schools for blacks in Prince Edward County were inferior to schools reserved for whites. The Defendants in this case were ordered to begin a program of equalization. The Plaintiffs' request for an injunction against school segregation was denied.

The law suit in the Delaware case was filed in the Delaware Court of Chancery requesting an injunction also against segregation in public schools. The Court concluded that the schools for blacks in New Castle County were inferior to those for whites and ordered that blacks be admitted immediately to schools previously reserved for whites only. The Supreme Court of Delaware reviewed the case and indicated that the order requiring integration was subject to modification after equalization of the schools.

The four school segregation cases were consolidated for disposition before a United States Supreme Court very much aware of the importance of the issues presented. The Court indicated, "Today, education is perhaps the most important function of state and local governments. Compulsory school attendance laws and the great expenditures for education both demonstrate our recognition of the importance of education to our democratic society. It is required in the performance of our most basic public responsibilities, even service in the armed forces. It is the very foundation of good citizenship. Today it is a principal instrument in awakening the child to cultural values, in preparing him for later professional training, and in helping him to adjust normally to his environment. In these days, it is doubtful that any child may reasonably be expected to succeed in life if he is denied the opportunity of an education."[33] The Court was conscious of the fact that its decision in the case would critically affect the quality of life in the United States for millions of Americans.

The Supreme Court referred to its previous observation in the Sweatt v Painter case that segregation deprived blacks of intangible considerations incapable of objective measurement. Also, the Court agreed with the assessment of the Kansas District Court that segregation created a feeling of inferiority in the hearts and minds of black students. The Court reached the conclusion that, "in the field of education the doctrine of separate but equal has no place. Separate educational facilities are inherently unequal."[34] Segregation in public education was declared unconstitutional.

The Supreme Court's 1954 school desegregation ruling greatly undermined the legal basis for forced segregation in general.[35] The actual abolition of forced segregation, however, in places of public accommodations and even in our public schools was a long and painful process that continued well into the 1960's. As a nation, we struggled painfully with our race relations until finally state compelled segregation was abandoned. Our struggle resulted also in the enactment of state and federal laws prohibiting racial discrimination in many important aspects of our lives.

Race-consciousness Continues

Tremendous strides have been made to remove the sanction of law from distinctions based on race. But, unfortunately, we are still continuing with many race-conscious practices. Our race-conscious ways of doing things and our race-conscious attitudes and perceptions in general are still with us. And race-consciousness today is every bit as real and, in many cases, just as detrimental as the racist practices that prevailed prior to the desegregation initiatives of the 1950's and 1960's.

Race-consciousness is continuing today in housing, social activities, the distribution of goods and services, jobs, occupations, movies, plays, art, literature, politics, the dissemination of news and other information, and in practically every aspect of our lives. Race-consciousness is continuing today as a very dominant factor in our society. And race-consciousness is continuing to preclude equality of treatment.

The practice of race-consciousness in the United States is so deeply entrenched that many people behave as though there is no other way for them to go about their affairs. Many people behave as though there is no personal choice in the matter whatsoever. Some people believe human beings are somehow compelled to jump up and down whenever there is a difference in skin color. As strange as it may seem to some, however, race-consciousness is not a necessary condition of life. Race-consciousness is a decision. We made the decision to develop as a race-conscious nation. We can also make the decision to abandon our race-conscious ways.

Poverty

Race-consciousness is one aspect of our racial problem. The other aspect is poverty. Millions of black Americans are impoverished today as a direct result of past racist practices. In 1984, 33.8 percent of the black people in our country lived in poverty. The percentage rate for whites was

11.5. During the period from 1969 to 1982, the poverty level for blacks remained above thirty percent. The poverty level for whites during that period did not exceed 12.2 percent. 41.8 percent of all blacks in our country lived in poverty in 1966. The poverty level for whites that year was 12.2.[36]

Poverty is a condition that traps and humiliates its victims and it does so without regard to race; and yet it affects blacks disproportionately. It affects blacks disproportionately because of our past. Blacks were released from slavery following the Civil War by Constitutional Amendment. But they were released without penny, property or education. They were released into the waiting arms of poverty. Moreover, from the time of Emancipation until well into the 1960's, blacks were prevented by unequal education, discrimination in employment, forced segregation, denial of voting rights and other discriminatory devices from improving their lives. Blacks were shot, lynched, beaten and degraded in every respect. An overall atmosphere of intimidation existed that prevented blacks from exercising even those rights permitted by law.

The elimination of past racist practices did not deliver blacks from poverty; nor did it put blacks in a position sufficient for them to deliver themselves.

It happens to be the case in our country that if you are born poor you will probably die poor, and your children will probably live in poverty as well. Very definite factors contribute to this unfortunate truth. Poor people are precluded by their financial situation from obtaining education and training sufficient to uplift them. More importantly, poor people are demoralized and discouraged by the physical, emotional and mental aspects of poverty. Feelings of frustration and hopelessness destroy ambitions and aspirations. Poor nutrition, bad housing, inadequate medical care and anxiety about daily affairs in general create apathy, indifference, resignation and family instability. The poor experience a high rate of crime and violence. They are preoccupied and overwhelmed by the very conditions in which they live. Children especially are affected by these conditions. They do not develop with sufficient hope or desire to improve their situation. They repeat the cycle of their parents.[37]

Blacks were forced into poverty by our past racist practices. They remain in poverty today because poverty is a condition from which, even without racism, there is essentially no escape.

Responsibility for Our Situation

The responsibility for the past that produced our current situation, both as to race-consciousness and black economic inequities, rests with the citizens of the United States collectively. Whether by racial assault, legislative action, the lack of corrective action, court decisions, or acquiescence, past racial injustices against blacks had the participation of our entire nation. The responsibility for our situation is ours, even though we did not personally participate in slavery, even though we may not have personally discriminated against blacks in any manner whatsoever, and even though some blacks themselves may be misguided in their attitudes and actions.

Responsibility for our situation is not absolved by the fact that it was our ancestors, and not us personally, who determined our past course with regard to race. We cannot divorce ourselves from our past. We did not personally participate in the drafting of the Constitution of the United States, and yet we claim the benefits of that document without hesitation. The Constitutional guarantees of freedom of religion, freedom of the press, free speech and the like are precious to us. We realize that our rich history in general is responsible for much of the prosperity we enjoy today. And we do proudly claim that prosperity. If we accept then the benefits of our past we should also accept its responsibilities.

Of course, acceptance of responsibility for our situation is not entirely a matter of choice. A problem has been thrust upon us. That much has been done. There is severity and detriment for all. Whether we have the will or capacity to get ourselves out of our predicament remains to be seen.

Part Two:
The Solution

CHAPTER 3

CURRENT EFFORTS INADEQUATE – SOME MISGUIDED

Current efforts against racial inequities in the United States consist essentially of laws prohibiting racial discrimination and specific initiatives to upgrade blacks in our society.

Provisions against governmental discrimination, state and federal, are contained in the Constitution of the United States. State discrimination is prohibited also by state constitutions. Provisions against the racist activities of individuals are embodied in state constitutions and state and federal civil rights statutes.

Federal civil rights legislation prohibits discrimination on the basis of race, color, religion or national origin in employment, programs or activities receiving federal financial assistance, and places and facilities of public accommodations. Racial segregation is also prohibited. Aggrieved individuals are allowed to make claims under federal law for remedies. The Attorney General of the United States is authorized also to act on behalf of victims.

Enforcement of federal provisions against discrimination in employment is the responsibility primarily of The Equal Employment Opportunity Commission of the federal government. Allegations of illegal practices are filed with the Commission. The Commission investigates complaints and attempts to eliminate unlawful practices with "informal methods of conference, conciliation and persuasion." The Commission is permitted, when informal methods fail, to file a law suit in federal court to compel compliance with the law. Victims of discrimination dissatisfied with the results of the Commission may, under certain circumstances, seek remedies in federal court on their own.[1]

State laws against racial discrimination are very similar to the federal civil rights provisions. State laws prohibit both segregation and discrimination in education, housing, public accommodations and employment. Complaints of racially discriminatory practices are filed with state agencies that, like the federal Equal Employment Opportunity Commission, investigate complaints and attempt to alleviate illegal activity by methods of conciliation. State agencies may also seek court enforcement. Victims of racist practices may, under certain circumstances, seek remedies on their own in state courts.[2]

Some racist activities are addressed by criminal law. It is a crime under federal law for "two or more persons" to "conspire to injure, oppress, threaten, or intimidate any citizens in the free exercise or enjoyment of any right or privilege secured to him by the Constitution or laws of the United States."[3] It is a federal crime as well for anyone under color of law to willfully deprive another, on the basis of race, of "any rights, privileges, or immunities secured or protected by the Constitution or laws of the United States."[4]

Criminal penalties are also imposed by state laws. It is a crime under some state laws, for example, for individuals to willfully interfere with state agencies charged with eliminating illegal discriminatory practices.[5]

Beyond the matter of prohibiting discriminatory practices, which by itself is certainly not a sufficient solution to our problems, current efforts to alleviate racial inequities are concentrated heavily in the areas of education and training, economic development and political participation.

There is a consensus of opinion, among those concerned about racial justice, that it is especially important for blacks to pursue education. Special efforts are made by state and federal agencies to educate black Americans. Efforts are made by the colleges and universities of our country to maintain an enrollment of black and other minority students. Also, the United Negro College Fund, the Office for Advancement of Public Black Colleges, the National Association for the Advancement of Black Americans in Vocational Education and many other organizations and individuals make special efforts to educate and train our black citizens.[6]

There is a consensus of opinion also that it is important for blacks to develop economically. Government policies designed to aid the development of black businesses have been adopted at both the state and federal levels. The federal Small Business Administration is required by statute, for example, to assist minority business concerns.[7] Agencies and offices have been established by various states to provide guidance and assistance to minority businesses.[8] Additionally, as is the case with black education and training, black economic development is promoted by many private individuals and organizations. To name only a few, black economic development is promoted by the National Black United Front of

Brooklyn, New York, the Council For A Black Economic Agenda of Washington, D.C., and the National Minority Business Campaign of Minneapolis, Minnesota.[9] Black Enterprise, a monthly magazine published by Earl G. Graves Publishing Company of New York City, addresses the concerns and needs of black businesses.

Political participation as a measure against racial inequities involves efforts to promote legislation that serves the needs and interest of the black community. Efforts are made also to register black voters and to elect political candidates favorable to black citizens.

Political concerns of blacks are addressed by the National Black Caucus of Local Elected Officials, the National Conference of Black Mayors, the National Black Caucus of State Legislators, The Congressional Black Caucus and by many other organizations and individuals.[10] Operation Big Vote, the National Coalition on Black Voter Participation and other organizations and individuals work specifically to increase black voter registration.[11]

The current approach against racial inequities, for blacks, is actually a continuation of the concept of black power. This concept developed initially, during the 1960's, out of a general feeling of frustration. Blacks became disillusioned in that the activities of the Civil Rights Movement had failed to produce true racial equality.

Black power advocates argued that blacks should strive to obtain rights and privileges from a position of economic and political strength, and not on the basis of morality alone. Blacks were urged to develop black communities for the benefit and control of black people. They were urged: 1) to organize within black communities for political power, 2) to elect representatives, 3) to force elected representatives to truly speak for the needs of black people, 4) to reject integration as a solution to black problems, 5) to work to see that money spent by blacks benefit the black community, and 6) to maintain black consciousness as a basis for political strength. Advocates of black power maintained that the needs of blacks would be adequately addressed only after blacks gained control over their own affairs. Black power advocates would accept coalitions with some whites on terms acceptable to blacks, but would not allow whites to participate in control over black lives.[12]

Interestingly, the gains of the Civil Rights Movement created an environment well suited for black power's evolvement. The policy of race-conscious affirmative action, initiated during the 1960's to help blacks advance in education, employment and business, was consistent with black power's notion of black economic development and black autonomy. The Voting Rights Act of 1965 permitted blacks to exercise the right to vote in the furtherance of black political power.

The basic ideas and beliefs of black power have persisted since the

1960's with great influence and persuasion among black people. Blacks today are continuing the pursuit of black economic and black political power.

Blacks today promote and advance the cause of black businesses. Black businesses employ black workers and produce profits for black entrepreneurs. The essential expectation is that blacks who are strong economically are in a position to obtain what they are entitled to with their buying power, and are therefore less dependent for their needs and wants on the discretion of racially motivated whites. There is an expectation also that the rights and privileges derived from black economic prosperity will give blacks greater overall participation in determining rules and practices governing their lives.

Additionally, blacks have the discretion, at least in principle, to refuse to buy goods or services from businesses that do not address black concerns. The expectation in this regard is that blacks can use their buying power to influence American businesses to adopt practices and policies favorable to black people.

The pursuit of black economic power has certainly contributed to black businesses and some black individuals. And the American business community is conscious of blacks as consumers. But black economic power has not evolved as a solution to our racial problem. Black economic power has not demonstrated the capacity to uplift the black masses from poverty or eliminate other racial inequities.

Black political power has also failed to evolve as a solution to our problem.

Black political power is derived essentially from a consensus in political opinion among black people. Blacks are induced by this consensus to vote in political elections with a common political sentiment, especially in those elections involving race or race-related issues. By voting together as a group, for or against political candidates, blacks have the power to play a tremendous role in the election of some public officials. And this power enables blacks to influence some officials in the implementation of policies and practices in the interest and concern of black people.

Black political power has been accepted by most American people. And what legitimate objection can there possibly be, one might ask, to special interest political participation by blacks in a democracy such as ours. The meshing of various ideas and concerns into ultimate political resolutions is precisely what the democratic process is all about. Also, American political decisions, whatever the role of blacks, are American political decisions.

Black political power is perceived by many Americans as just another special interest group. And there is a prevailing confidence that the American people have the unique capacity, within the American political system, to accommodate various political pressures, ideas, interests, and concerns. There is a confidence that the American people cannot be overpowered, misled, or intimidated by black political participation.

Black political power has not motivated the American people to resolve continuing racial inequities. The American people are basically accommodating black political power without discarding their racial attitudes or practices.

The current organization and affiliation of blacks unto themselves, despite the limitations of black economic and black political power, is very very extensive. We have numerous black businesses. We have black newspapers; black magazines; black radio stations; black political, social, business, economic, recreational, student and public interest organizations; and black institutions of all sorts. Blacks today organize and affiliate unto themselves to provide separately for their own educational, social, psychological and recreational needs. Blacks are functioning today, to a great extent, as a separate and distinct entity with an allegiance, culture and outlook of their own.

The separate development of blacks in the pursuit of black power as a method to eliminate racial inequities has been in place now for a period of more than twenty years. It has not moved us in the direction of true racial equality. In fact, it has contributed to the hardening of harmful racial attitudes. The separate development of blacks in the pursuit of black power is not the solution to our problem.

Separate black development does not recognize the importance of white participation in the fight against racial inequities. Indeed, white participation is discouraged, and in some respects, altogether precluded, by the very principles of the concept of black power. The concept of black power is in essence an endorsement of the terribly misguided concept that whites ought not to be involved in the pursuit of racial justice.

But white participation in the efforts against racial inequities is essential. And this truth is clearly supported by the events of our past. The two major racial achievements in our history, the abolition of slavery and the abandonment of state compelled segregation, were accomplished not by blacks alone, but by blacks and whites working together.

Participation by white Americans prior to the Civil War in activities against slavery is well documented. John Q. Adams, after serving as President of the United States from 1825 to 1829, waged a long battle (from 1831 to 1848) against slavery in the United States House of Representatives.[13] William Lloyd Garrison campaigned against slavery in his newspaper, The Liberator, and helped also in the founding of the American Anti-Slavery Society in 1833.[14] Abolitionist John Brown conducted acts of violence against slavery and was in fact hanged to death as a result of an attack in 1859 on an armory at Harpers Ferry, Virginia.[15]

John Wesley of the Methodist Church publicly opposed slavery in 1774.[16] Editor William Swain addressed the people of North Carolina in 1830 on the evils of slavery.[17] Also in 1830, citizens of Maine petitioned the Senate of the United States to eliminate slavery in the Nation's capitol.[18]

Many white individuals and organizations not mentioned here also made contributions against slavery. White Americans established numerous local and national abolitionist societies and promoted vigorously the anti-slavery ambitions of those organizations.[19] Slavery in the United States was abolished by the determined efforts of both blacks and whites.

Whites participated heavily also in the Civil Rights Movement of the 1950's and 1960's. For example, approximately 60,000 whites were among the 250,000 citizens who marched on the Nation's capitol in 1963. White participation in activities to repudiate laws and practices requiring racial segregation was significant. Whites and blacks worked together. Whites and blacks lost their lives. The success of the Civil Rights Movement was due to multiracial activity against racist practices. Blacks alone certainly would not have done as well.

There is no mystery or magic as to why multiracial activity is effective. Racism stands strong against the efforts of blacks alone. A perception is created that our racial situation is nothing more than a confrontation between blacks and whites. Citizens are prevented by this misguided perception from even considering the issue of equality of treatment. All is perceived simply as a matter of blacks fighting whites.

Participation by blacks and whites together increases the number of people engaged in anti-racist activities. The effort against racial inequities gains in strength and momentum. Blacks alone are not sufficient in number or political or economic strength to impose racial solutions on the people of the United States. If racial solutions are to be implemented, many many white Americans must somehow be persuaded to acquiesce. There is simply no way to avoid it. And blacks and whites together can do a far better job in persuading whites on racial issues than blacks alone.

One might take the position that reliance on multiracial activity conveys the impression that blacks are incompetent and incapable of doing things without the help of whites. Enlisting the aid of whites, some may argue, promotes the idea of white supremacy. As previously stated, however, blacks now have an uplifted sense of pride and self-confidence. The fact that skin color does not confer superiority is now firmly established in the minds and hearts of our black citizens. Multiracial activity is no longer a question of self-confidence or racial pride, but rather a matter of reason and common sense.

Opposition to multiracial activity on the basis of black pride would be an indication of confusion as to the true nature of our problem. The racial problem in the United States is due largely to attitudes and beliefs held by whites. Thus, unless whites are going to vanish from the face of the earth or suddenly become incapacitated, they must indeed be a part of any racial solution. As a practical matter, there is no way for blacks alone to solve our problem.

It is important also to abandon the attitude that any action to eliminate racial inequities should be initiated by blacks. Whites should also take initiatives. The racial problem in the United States is not the property of black people. It belongs equally to blacks and whites. Whites are not insulated from the harmful consequences of our racial situation. In fact, whites have far more to lose than blacks. What can the black masses possibly lose? Their lives have already been claimed by poverty, crime, and racial humiliation. Whites today must adopt the cause against racial inequities as their own. After all, it is their own. It belongs to all of us.

The current approach to our racial problem is wrong for the reason also that harmful racial attitudes are not being adequately addressed. Separate black development calls on blacks essentially to promote the interests of blacks. But the advancement of blacks without the elimination of harmful attitudes would leave much of our racial problem unresolved. The best that one can reasonably expect from separate black development is the maintenance, enlargement, and enrichment of the black middle class. Racial inequities would continue. Even the advancement of every black individual in the United States would not, by itself, eliminate racially derogatory treatment. Racial insults, racial hatred and racial violence would still be with us.

The idea that black achievement alone will destroy racist perceptions is a fallacy. A black person who excels in science, for example, may become a great black scientist, perhaps the best scientist ever, but still a black scientist. No matter how great the achievement, a black person will always be a black person; and what it means to be black will continue to be defined by American attitudes as derogatory for as long as we maintain our current level of race-consciousness.

It would be wrong to take the position that racist perceptions are unimportant if blacks are allowed certain advancements. As a practical matter, black advancement would never really be secure in a hostile racial environment. But even if it could be made secure in such an environment, which it cannot, there would still be hurt and pain precipitated by racist attitudes. Successful blacks are not immune to insult. Derogatory treatment is very very real and can be devastating even when not accompanied by the denial of legal rights or political or economic opportunities. Racial insult is the very essence of racism. An approach to our problem that accommodates that awful indignity ought not to be acceptable.

CHAPTER 4

STRONG EFFECTIVE POLICY AGAINST RACIAL DISCRIMINATION

If we are to adequately address the racial problem in the United States, we must first reach the conclusion as a nation that racism is wrong. There are clear indications today, especially in the occurrence of recent racial confrontations, that we have unfortunately not reached that conclusion. For example, certain whites in Philadelphia in 1985 were angered and outraged that blacks moved into "their" neighborhood. Some whites in that neighborhood organized and conducted protest activities against their black neighbors, and felt very righteous indeed about their actions.[1] In 1986, whites dressed as members of the white racist Klu Klux Klan organization confronted a black cadet at the Citadel in South Carolina. Also in 1986, blacks were chased by whites at the University of Massachusetts-Amherst. In 1987, hundreds of whites motivated by racism attacked an interracial group of citizens in Forsyth County, Georgia.[2] In 1989, a racist group calling itself Americans for a Competent Federal Judicial System claimed responsibility for bombings that killed a federal judge and a civil rights lawyer.[3] These incidents and others are symptoms of deep rooted and perhaps widespread racial resentment that should be of great concern to us.

People organize today to show their racial hatred. Assaults motivated by racism are designed, calculated and carried out with a strong sense of righteousness and purpose. Some people are being persuaded, perhaps by daily activities and conversations in their neighborhoods, that it is good and proper to engage in racial hatred. Some misguided citizens may even sense tacit approval of racism in the character of public condemnation of racist activities. Public condemnation has not been as extensive or as severe as circumstances have warranted.

To what extent does the feeling exist that it is good to hate and discriminate on the basis of skin color? To what extent do we believe racism is wrong, but not all that bad? How widespread is racial resentment? The actual extent of racial animosity is something nobody really knows. But we do know we have a problem. And it is important that we act now to forcefully, thoroughly and unequivocally reject racism anywhere and everywhere it exists throughout the United States.

Let us go right to the heart of our problem and impose the requirement on our grammar schools, elementary schools, high schools, trade schools, colleges and universities that our students be taught in civic and social courses that racism is wrong, and that all our citizens have a right to be treated equally and in a courteous and dignified manner. Courses would be designed to deliver this important message without promoting race-consciousness. This can be accomplished by simply teaching our students what our laws, policies and values are regarding discrimination, not only as to race, but also as to religion, sex and national origin. Education courses would examine both state and federal policies. Students would be introduced to specific provisions of state and federal civil rights laws. Applicable provisions of the Constitution of the United States would be taught. State constitutional provisions would also be explored.

The education requirements recommended here should be implemented at state and local levels, rather than by the federal government. State and local requirements on courses of study are already in place. Students are already required to take courses in mathematics, science, history and other areas.

Some school courses today are specifically required by state laws. Typically, however, the authority to prescribe courses in public schools is delegated by states to local school boards or to other local authorities.[4] In the case of colleges and universities, delegation is to boards of trustees and other governing entities.

The power of states to prescribe courses in public schools is fundamental. State power to participate in setting course requirements at private schools exists in the power of states to license, accredit and tax. License privileges, tax exempt status and/or accreditation can be withheld from those private schools that do not abide by state wishes.

The teaching of our laws and values with regard to racial discrimination is of such importance that it should be required specifically by state laws in all public and private schools, at both the primary and secondary levels, and also at colleges and universities. Specific course requirements should be set. Procedures should be established to insure that courses are implemented and maintained with integrity.

The message that racism is wrong must be sounded not only in our classrooms, but also on our streets and indeed in every household. Our efforts in this regard should involve the placement of a public opinion referendum on ballots affirming our belief in equality of treatment. A referendum statement would read, for example, "All citizens of the United States are entitled to be treated in an equal and dignified manner in every aspect of life, and should be afforded equal protection under our laws, without regard to race, sex, religion or national origin."

The referendum would be placed on ballots in consolidation with the regular election of legislators, governors, mayors and other public officials. This process would not impinge on individual rights. At polling stations, voters could ignore the referendum altogether. A voter who elects to participate, however, would vote "no" to disavow the referendum statement or "yes" to adopt the statement as his or her own personal belief.

During the months immediately preceding each election, civil rights organizations, public officials and others would remind the American people to affirm their beliefs in our laws and policies. Voters would be urged not to abstain and efforts would be made also to register and involve unregistered voters in the referendum process. The referendum process would function to overpower racist ideas and attitudes. The misguided would be educated as to the true policy of our nation. Existing beliefs in equality of treatment would be affirmed and reinforced. Our nation would be reminded of its commitment to all of its citizens.

The referendum process would benefit us also in that the voting results would tell us what people feel and think about racial discrimination. This information would guide us in determining on a continuous basis what policies should be maintained in the best interest of all our citizens.

The proposed opinion referendum would be implemented by state law. The polling process in the United States, like the setting of school course requirements, is managed at the state level. State statutes would require that the referendum be placed on the ballot in all voting districts in consolidation with regularly scheduled elections of public officials.

The opinion referendum has been firmly established as an acceptable way for government to attend to its affairs. It is allowed, for example, by the State of California on issues of interest in local elections.[5] Referendums on illegal discrimination would serve our nation well in securely establishing the policy not only that racism is wrong, but also that it is completely and totally unacceptable.

A strong policy against racial discrimination would require also that we ask our public officials, at all levels, to make periodic public statements affirming their beliefs in our laws and values regarding equality of treatment and equal opportunity for all. Much can be done by public officials in speeches, proclamations and news conferences to implement, maintain, and promote a vigorous policy against illegal and improper discrimination. While it may be improper for public officials to comment on specific incidents of racism where criminal or civil court action is involved or anticipated, we should nevertheless expect and demand strong denunciation of racism in general in times of racial confrontations.

Alliances among public officials should also be developed and suggestions derived therefrom on the contents and frequency of public announcements against illegal discrimination. Public officials can make great contributions to improve our race relations simply by speaking out against racism. Public officials must speak out. After all, if one truly believes in equality of treatment, he or she ought not to be afraid to say so. Those who may be a bit reluctant to speak out could perhaps be persuaded by public demonstrations or other appropriate tactics. Individuals aspiring to obtain or retain elected positions could be pressured during election campaigns.

Strong advertisement campaigns directly against racism should be used as well. Civil rights organizations and others should pool finances for the purpose of conducting such campaigns. An alliance of organizations and individuals could be formed to raise funds and manage certain activities. Advertisement campaigns would be used to affirm the American belief in equality of treatment with the same vigor and imagination used by today's businesses to sell products and services. Celebrities would be used to make public statements. Blacks and whites would be shown living and working together. Positive messages would be developed for television, radio, newspapers, and magazines.

It is important that our policy against racism go no further than to teach and affirm our laws and values. Efforts against racist practices should not argue that blacks are worthy people. The worthiness of blacks is not debatable.

Also, although our policy against racist practices would involve specific messages against racism, our attack in general, whether in our schools, on our streets, or in our households, would be against all illegal and improper discrimination. It would be a mistake to address the issue of race alone. The pursuit of racial issues only would unnecessarily promote race-consciousness. Also, attention to other forms of disparate treatment would present an opportunity for all Americans who face discrimination in the United States to work together for a common good.

CHAPTER 5

POLICY AGAINST RACE-CONSCIOUSNESS

The resolution of our racial problem will also require the implementation of a policy against race-consciousness. The development of such a policy probably would have been precluded in the past by existing race-conscious attitudes themselves. Today, however, that policy can be formulated. Indeed, it must be formulated and thoroughly and vigorously promoted.

The prohibition of racially discriminatory conduct is certainly the right thing to do. But racial discrimination is but a symptom of the diseased feelings and attitudes we embrace. We must treat the diseased feelings and attitudes from which racially discriminatory conduct originates. There can be no cure until we cure our inner- selves. We must destroy that element within us that makes us act in a manner demeaning and detrimental to others solely on the basis of skin color. We must work to make race an unimportant consideration in all aspects of our lives.

Of course, misguided thoughts and beliefs cannot be eliminated simply by enacting laws that make them illegal, and no attempt in this regard should even be contemplated. Certain adjustments, however, can be made. Impediments to positive developments can be removed. Healthy ideas and beliefs can be promoted.

Separate Black Development

An effective policy against race-consciousness would involve the discontinuance of separate black development. Separate black development should be discontinued, not by legislation or other governmental action prohibiting its existence, but by convincing blacks and whites to give it up voluntarily. An effort must be made to persuade the citizens of our country that the maintenance of black separatism in the United States today is a mistake.

Of course, some people feel separate black development is crucial for the advancement of black people. Some people feel special efforts must be made to secure benefits and opportunities solely for black Americans. There is an opinion that our racial situation would not allow the fair treatment of blacks in open competition and association with whites. There is an opinion also that separate black development functions in general as a sanctuary where blacks are afforded relief from oppressive race-conscious attitudes and practices.

Separate black development does indeed secure opportunities for black people. And it does in fact allow blacks to withdraw from the cruelties of our situation. It creates opportunities for blacks to associate with blacks. It recognizes the achievements of black individuals. It functions actually to maintain a society unto itself in which blacks are permitted to compete solely with other blacks for prestige, recognition, employment and other opportunities.

To persist, however, with the competition of blacks among blacks is to allow unfair treatment in open competition to continue. Inequitable practices will not be changed without a challenge. And there will be no challenge so long as blacks keep unto themselves.

Separate black development is detrimental also in that it restricts the expectations and achievements of black individuals. Blacks are motivated to become the highest black elected official, the best black teacher, the best black scientist, and the like, rather than the best overall. There is a disincentive for blacks to reach for opportunities beyond set asides and established expectations.

The discontinuance of separate black development is not something we should be afraid to do. Separate black development must be abandoned, notwithstanding the fact that black togetherness has been a source of tremendous strength over the years for blacks to carry on the fight for equality of treatment. Togetherness would not be lost. The sense of togetherness that provides strength and determination against racist practices need not and should not be on the basis of race; rather, it should be on the basis of commitment to the goal of racial equality.

Furthermore, black separatism contributes to the erroneous perception that all whites are enemies of blacks. Such is not the case. Racism, and not white people, is the evil about which we ought to be concerned. The exclusion of whites does not secure blacks against racist practices. In fact, it makes blacks less secure. There is greater strength in the togetherness of people of all races, religions and backgrounds than in the togetherness of blacks alone. Commitment to justice and fair treatment, and not to the color of one's skin, should be the common bond.

Black Culture

There may be concern on the part of some that the abandonment of separate black development would destroy the black culture. And it is indeed the intention of the recommendations being made here to destroy race-consciousness wherever it exists. Change is the recommendation. But change in culture is not necessarily bad. Slavery and forced racial segregation certainly made contributions in the past to the black culture, and yet blacks are not at all disappointed that those horrible practices have now been abolished. Poverty contributes today to the black culture but few would insist for the sake of culture that poverty be continued. Thus, we should not hesitate to eliminate race-consciousness from our culture, if by such an elimination, we can truly move closer to our goal of equality of treatment for all.

Black Pride

There may be some concern also that the abandonment of separate black development would result in a detriment to the pride, self-respect and confidence of our black citizens. There is no question that race-consciousness has served to enhance the self-esteem of blacks by promoting positive images of black people. Racist attitudes were so oppressive in the past that the promotion of positive images was undoubtedly the necessary and proper thing to do. But race is just not the proper foundation, certainly not today, upon which to build personal character.

An individual who relies on skin color as a measure of his or her worth is in a position of great vulnerability. If black skin means one is worthy, then everyone with black skin should be worthy. Thus, self-esteem built on black racial pride is threatened whenever there is discredit to even one black individual. In the interest of self-confidence, some blacks often feel compelled to defend, justify, distinguish or explain the unscrupulous actions of other black individuals. What an awesome burden! It is an impossible task. But if we pay far less attention to matters of race, there would be no foundation for attacks on blacks as a group; and the self-esteem of blacks would be allowed to develop on an individual basis, the way it should be, unimpeded by negative racial perceptions.

Black Organizations

The abandonment of separate black development would involve the discontinuance of black organizations and affiliations, many that were established in the aftermath of the emergence of the concept of black power. Of course, some black organizations were in existence and involved in efforts against racist practices long before the events of the 1960's. For example, the National Association for Advancement of Colored People (NAACP) was established in the year 1909. The NAACP has won numerous political, legal and social opportunities for our black citizens.[1] The National Urban League is another example. The National Urban League has worked continuously since 1911 to gain opportunities for blacks in businesses and industries. The National Urban League works also to provide housing opportunities and guidance and counseling.[2]

Black organizations in our country have a very special history and tradition. They are heavily relied on to improve the quality of life for our black citizens. They have been a source of strength and encouragement for millions. The men and women involved in black organizations have made extraordinary efforts against racism. They have made tremendous sacrifices to improve our race relations. They are moved by love, determination and commitment. They give their time and indeed their lives in the pursuit of racial equality.

The positive contributions of black organizations cannot be questioned. As a result of those contributions, our country is a better place in which to live. But black organizations today sanction and reinforce the great attention we give to matters of race. They contribute to the harmful perception that the affairs of blacks are to be managed separately from the affairs of whites.

That which serves well at one particular time does not necessarily serve well indefinitely. No matter how great the service, occasionally there comes a time for change. The time for change with regard to black organizations is now. There is a point beyond which black organizations cannot effectively carry the fight for racial equality. The torch must be passed on. We should turn now to civil rights organizations developed on a truly multiracial basis to finally resolve our racial problem.

Organizations against racial inequities should be maintained, not as black organizations, but as multiracial organizations, and therefore should not include words such as black, colored, negro or minority in their names or titles. Organizations against racial inequities should represent all victims of racial discrimination and victims of other illegal discriminatory practices as well. Civil rights organizations must reach out to get whites, blacks and people of all races and backgrounds involved in their efforts (as members and as friends).

Some black organizations today do enjoy some white participation and support. But that is not enough. Organizations against racial inequities should not operate at all as black or minority entities, and should reject any and all efforts to portray them as such.

The discontinuance of black organizations would not adversely affect the fight against racial inequities. In fact, the quest for racial equality would be enhanced. A multiracial legislative caucus against racial inequities, for example, would be much stronger and would have a far broader base than a legislative black caucus. Student organizations against racism would be far more effective than black student organizations. We should rely not on black organizations, but on organizations committed to equality of treatment.

Multiracial organizations would result in greater participation by whites against racial inequities. Opportunities must be created for blacks and whites to work together for racial equality. Whites are not inclined to believe such opportunities exist in black organizations. After all, black organizations are black organizations. All barriers that discourage or deter white participation in the pursuit of racial justice must be removed.

Of course, the elimination of black organizations alone would not guarantee greater white participation. Nor would it guarantee diminished race-consciousness. But the elimination of black organizations is not the only action being recommended. The recommendations being made here in their entirety address the overall attitudes and practices of both blacks and whites. The abandonment of race-consciousness would not be unilateral.

The discontinuance of black organizations would not make blacks more vulnerable to racist attacks. Blacks would still have the power to defend themselves. The ability to assemble and organize would not be impaired. Citizens would still come together to oppose racial injustices. But they would come together now on a multiracial basis. Multiracial efforts against racist attacks would be far more effective than the efforts of blacks alone.

Race-conscious Affirmative Action

An effective policy against race-consciousness would also require that we discard the policy of race-conscious affirmative action. Race-conscious affirmative action involves specific efforts to place blacks in schools, jobs and other positions without which the blacks so placed would presumably be excluded. Race is the primary consideration although the individuals involved must certainly be qualified.

Race-conscious affirmative action has been implemented by states, cities, towns and the federal government. It has been implemented by private employers and by other private entities. It has been formulated in court consent decrees and also required by court order.

Race-conscious affirmative action is a highly controversial policy. It has been challenged continuously in our courts and elsewhere since its very inception. It is a policy, nevertheless, that has been approved by the Supreme Court of the United States.

Race-conscious affirmative action was approved by the Supreme Court in the admission of students to state educational institutions in

1978 in the case of University of California Regents v Bakke.[3] The implementation of affirmative action by private employers was approved by the Court in 1979 in the case of Steelworkers v Weber.[4] Affirmative action was allowed to stand in a court consent decree in the 1986 case of Local Number 93 v City of Cleveland.[5] Court ordered affirmative action was approved by the Supreme Court in 1987 in the case of United States v Paradise.[6]

Opponents of race-conscious affirmative action have taken the position that the preferential treatment of blacks, involved in the disputed policy, discriminates against whites in violation of both the Civil Rights Act of 1964 and the Equal Protection Clause of the Fourteenth Amendment to the Constitution of the United States.

It is difficult to believe, here in the United States, that discrimination against whites, in favor of blacks, is a problem of any measurable proportion. But the rights of innocent whites cannot be ignored. The awesome burden of eliminating the Nation's racial inequities should in fact not be placed on individuals at all. Fundamental fairness would seem to require that efforts be made to place the burden on the American people collectively. After all, the responsibility for our racial situation rests not with individual citizens, but with our nation as a whole.

The United States Supreme Court has concluded as a matter of statutory interpretation that race-conscious efforts are permissible under the Civil Rights Act to correct racial imbalances. The Supreme Court has concluded also that affirmative action does not violate the Fourteenth Amendment. The Court has indicated, however, that race-conscious efforts are subject to close scrutiny and must be fair and reasonable. Some race-conscious efforts have been disallowed.[7]

The Supreme Court's conclusion that race-conscious affirmative action, if appropriately applied, does not violate the Fourteenth Amendment would appear to be justified, and perhaps even compelled, by the Constitution's past participation in race-consciousness. The Constitution of the United States, as interpreted by the Supreme Court, allowed states and individuals to maintain racial segregation in our country from the 1890's until well into the 1950's. Past segregation in schools, jobs and places of public accommodations is one of the primary reasons why racial inequities are with us today. It would be outrageously hypocritical for the Supreme Court to rule, as a matter of Constitutional law, that race may not now be used in policies to remedy wrongs in which the Constitution itself played a vital role. It is good that our Supreme Court has declined to perpetrate such a hypocrisy. Race-conscious affirmative action must be abandoned, but not on the basis of Constitutional law.

Many who support race-conscious affirmative action believe race-conscious efforts are essential, not only to correct racial inequities caused by past discrimination, but also as a shield against racial practices that continue today. In the opinion of some, race-conscious affirmative action has both a moral and legal justification. As a practical matter, however, race-conscious efforts are extremely harmful and ought to be abandoned voluntarily.

Race-conscious affirmative action and other race-conscious efforts put blacks and whites in direct competition with each other, on the basis of race, and thus serve to promote racial animosity. Race-conscious efforts promote racial hatred, racial resentment, racial jealousy and other racist feelings and attitudes. They contribute to an increased intolerance and disregard for the rights of blacks. They contribute to the hardening or racist attitudes.

Race-conscious affirmative action and other race-conscious efforts function also as instruments of racial misconceptions. They have convinced some Americans that blacks are responsible for the denial of opportunities to whites, that blacks are pursuing their own self interest only, without regard for the legitimate concerns and rights of others, that blacks are receiving advantages and privileges they do not rightfully deserve, and that whites and not blacks are the true victims of our race relations.[8]

One might take the position that the responsibility for racial animosities and racial misconceptions should be attributed, not to affirmative action, which is totally and completely justified, but solely to those individuals embracing such animosities and misconceptions. One might take the position that it is wrong to ask victims to make sacrifices to get the misguided to discard ideas and beliefs they ought not to have in the first place. The point can also be made that race-conscious remedies are not, by the stretch of anyone's imagination, solely responsible for today's racist beliefs and misconceptions.

All things considered, however, one must face the fact that race-conscious affirmative action and other race-conscious efforts serve the interest of racism far better than they do the cause against racial inequities.

Today's effort against racial inequities is conceding much too much in American public opinion. America does not sympathize as it should with the struggle for racial equality. Blacks have suffered tremendously as a result of our racial practices. And racial inequities continue. The fight for racial equality should be more favorably received by the American people. The rebuff of race-conscious affirmative action and other race-conscious efforts in American public opinion cannot be ignored. Race-conscious affirmative action and other race-conscious efforts are functioning, like black organizations, to dissuade individuals otherwise inclined to support the cause for racial justice.

The idea of using race-conscious measures to force people to do what is right is certainly understandable. After all, people should do what is right on their own. And if they do not, then they ought to be compelled. But, as previously indicated, any successful campaign against racial inequities, which does not overpower or incapacitate individuals with harmful attitudes, must ultimately change the hearts and minds of those individuals. And if people are going to change, they must become motivated to do so. Elements that operate as obstructions to change must be removed.

A policy against misguided ideas and beliefs would not be an indignity. It would not be wrong or improper to remove obstacles to better race relations. It would not be wrong or improper to point the way to more appropriate human behavior. No one would be asking that people suddenly become endeared to blacks. Who people like or dislike would remain a matter of personal taste and conscience. The recommendations being made here would simply provide direction for those individuals who, except for misguidance, would not have harmful racial attitudes any way. Of course, those individuals with depraved hearts and minds would probably be lost, but they would be lost in any case and no matter what.

The discontinuance of race-conscious affirmative action would not mean we would then ignore jobs, professions or other situations where blacks are excluded or have minimal participation. We would continue to look into those circumstances. We would work aggressively to provide remedies to individuals harmed by racism. We would criminally prosecute individuals who violate our criminal laws.

Fear that the abandonment of race-conscious affirmative action would result in the unfair exclusion of blacks from certain opportunities is not a sufficient reason to continue with race-consciousness. Proof of racial discrimination in employment and other areas does indeed depend, in many cases, on the subjective views of judges, juries and others in decision making capacities. But one ought not to adopt the pessimistic view that racism will dominate the hearts of our citizens, and defeat the stated purpose of our laws and policies. If our situation is such that we cannot have confidence that our government, laws, and people will be fair, then race-conscious affirmative action is hardly a sufficient solution.

Contrary to what some may think, race-conscious affirmative action is not essential to the survival of black people. We should be reminded that this controversial practice is a relatively new national policy. Blacks have survived and achieved in the face of great adversity for many many years without it. Also, although race-conscious affirmative action has been of benefit to some blacks, it has done little to improve the lives of the black masses. Poverty, poor housing conditions, low income, and unemployment continue to be major problems for our black citizens.

The subject here is race-conscious affirmative action. Affirmative action based on considerations other than race may be appropriate in certain situations. In fact, limited affirmative action should be available, without regard to race, color or creed, to persons of impoverished backgrounds. It should be applied in the admission of students to schools, colleges, universities, trade schools, professional schools and training programs, but not as to employment. With sufficient education and training, the poor should be able to compete successfully for jobs on their own.

Other Race-Conscious Practices

Other race-conscious practices must also be abandoned. Artistic endeavors by and/or about black people should not be recognized as black art, black music, black dance, or the like. The arts should certainly continue to deal with black people and issues involving race. But segregation in perception or otherwise solely on the basis of skin color ought not to be our practice.

The history in our country involving blacks should not be taught in a separate course as black history. It should be thoroughly integrated as part of our American history, which it is, and introduced to our students as such.

The special recognition of the achievements of black individuals, including attention to the first black to accomplish a certain goal, should be discontinued. Individuals, whether white or black, should be recognized for their accomplishments without regard to race.

The common use of racial statistics in the dissemination of information should be also discontinued. The use of racial statistics, even when with good intentions, leads too frequently to harmful and degrading results. Of special note are statistics that show a high incidence of certain maladies among blacks, particularly as to those maladies that are peculiar to the poor and have a high incidence among all poor whether black or white. Maladies of the poor affect blacks disproportionately because a disproportionate number of blacks live in poverty. This truth, however, is often lost and the impression is conveyed that blacks have certain maladies simply because they are black. Lost is the truth that poverty and not skin color is the determining factor. Lost is the fact that blacks were forced into poverty by the race-conscious practices of our country. Racial statistics do serve, in some cases, to mislead the American people. They should be used only when necessary and in every case with a clear and proper purpose.

We must relinquish our reliance on race-consciousness in every respect. A general awareness must be created as to its harmful consequences. Race-consciousness has not thus far been appreciated as an evil. Special attention to race, even if favorable or seemingly of no consequence, creates an overall harmful result and should be abandoned in all cases, except in those situations where race is in fact properly an issue.

CHAPTER 6

IN OUR EVERYDAY LIVES AS THOUGH RACE IS UNIMPORTANT

The discontinuance of race-consciousness will require additionally that blacks and whites behave in every respect in their everyday lives as though race is truly unimportant. Blacks especially must behave in such a fashion. After all, race will never ultimately become an unimportant consideration in American life until blacks themselves treat it as such. Moreover, blacks who behave as though race is unimportant will make it difficult, if not altogether impossible, for whites to treat them otherwise.

Blacks and whites can in fact take considerations of race out of their lives, even though we are at this time, as a whole, a race-conscious people. Blacks and whites must simply resist any and all temptations to interject race into their affairs. And they must positively withstand, on a case-by-case basis, those incidents of race-consciousness instigated or promoted by others.

Race Interjection

The interjection of race into our daily affairs, in many instances, involves direct or indirect submissions as to the worthiness of black people. But race-conscious activity intended to establish that blacks are worthy, when in fact black worthiness should not even be an issue, concedes much too much to evil presumptions and suggestions that blacks are less deserving than whites. Blacks are entitled to all the rights, privileges and respect afforded to others. Any outlook or posture to the contrary is an insult and a degradation to black people.

(Bill and Susan attend a local town meeting. The meeting adjourns and they

find themselves involved at the town hall in a very delightful conversation with another couple. A spirited middle-aged woman who had actively participated in the town meeting approaches and listens in. She manages to introduce herself as Margaret and asks Bill and Susan if they are the blacks who live on West Street. Bill assures her that they are not. Margaret then replies, "Well, a black family lives over there, and I've been trying to meet them.")

Whites who indicate at work, social affairs and other functions, public and private, that they have black friends or have had other positive experiences with black individuals are actually trying to show they are not prejudiced against black people. But why do they feel the need to make such a showing? To make a special point of it is to suggest some difficulty.

Race-conscious activity intended to establish that blacks are worthy serves to actually debate the issue. And to debate the issue is to concede that the issue is debatable. But the issue is not debatable and no concession in this regard ought to be made.

Also, blacks and whites should refrain, in daily conversations and occurrences, from presenting the "black perspective" on the various issues and matters affecting their lives.

(John is having lunch with co-workers. The topic of conversation is skiing. John makes the statement, "Well, I'm not a skier. You know, it used to be that not many blacks got involved in skiing. Now-a-days, more and more blacks are getting involved.")

"Blacks would never do that," "blacks don't feel that way," "it's different with blacks" and other similar assertions are ill-advised race-conscious generalizations. These generalizations are offered, in many cases, to bolster the esteem of blacks or to justify blacks in their expectations and stature. But there is no need to prove blacks are worthy. And there is no need to establish special justification for the lives of black people.

The interjection of race to deal with uneasy situations is also wrong.

(John is asked to make some brief remarks at the retirement dinner of a very popular co-worker. Many people attend and John, understandably, is a bit nervous. His initial comments, "If I appear a bit nervous tonight, it's because I am. I don't see many black people out there. I get a little nervous when I don't see black people.")

Additionally, race ought not to be interjected into non racial matters for the misguided purpose of distinguishing black individuals from whites. To distinguish blacks is to assume that there is just cause for such a distinction. And therein lies the degradation. "Mary is a black nurse," "Bill is a black mechanic," "John is a black who works in our payroll department" and similar race-conscious offerings should be avoided.

Of course, skin color is pertinent in some situations. It could be important, for example, in matters of physical description.

("I'm a medium built man, coffee bean color, about six feet tall, hundred and eighty pounds, short hair, moustache, and I'll wait for you right out in front of the building.")

But physical descriptions should be specific. Race-conscious generalizations can still be avoided.

Also, there is certainly no intent here to preclude legitimate public or private discussion about the racial issues affecting our lives. If race is a legitimate issue, then it ought to be considered. In most situations, however, indications of race are of little or no benefit to anything except the promotion of race-consciousness.

Withstanding The Race-Consciousness Conduct Of Others

Withstanding the race-conscious conduct of others is a matter largely of refusing to be drawn into race-conscious activity. Race-conscious acts intended to insult, deny, or otherwise harm, or instigated with arrogance or reckless disregard for the rights of others, or instigated even without the intent to harm cannot be allowed to compromise the spirit and attitude that race is unimportant.

Some race-conscious activity can and should be handled by a simple disregard of the particular race-conscious conduct involved. One would disregard a race-conscious comment, for example, simply by not responding to it, and allowing the topic of conversation to move on to other matters. An individual may choose to even direct a conversation to other matters. One may elect also to just walk away from the situation.

(Denise is at her desk at a new office job. A co-worker who had been previously introduced walks over to talk. During the course of the conversation: Co-worker, "Did I tell you we have blacks in our neighborhood? A black Doctor and his family moved in. And then there's another black family. I don't know what they do." Denise, "You know what? The health benefits? I don't know which plan to enroll in. What plan do you have?")

(Don is in the rest room at a local bar. He washes his hands at the sink and dries them with paper towels. A burly man is standing nearby. The man, "It doesn't wash off." Don, "What did you say?" The man, "The color. It doesn't

wash off." Without another word, Don adjusts his pants, checks himself in the mirror and leaves the rest room.)

(Carl is taking a chartered bus to Atlantic City. He is to meet with others in the lobby of a prominent hotel. He enters the lobby past the hotel attendant. People are already there waiting. Among them is Henry, an acquaintance. Henry calls out jokingly to Carl, "Hey, blacks are not allowed in here. Didn't they tell you that?" Carl moves over to the group. Henry goes on, "Don't you know blacks are not allowed in here?")

In the above described incident in the hotel lobby, what would be the proper response? Should Carl respond in kind in a jokingly manner? He could respond, for example, "What year is this? I thought for a moment I was back in the 1950's, down in the deep south some place." But Henry's conduct should not be accommodated. Accommodation would be undignified and too great a concession to race-consciousness.

Carl may feel obliged as a matter of personal human dignity to confront Henry immediately. But confrontation need not involve a verbal exchange. To disregard is a form of confrontation. And in some situations, the disregard of race-conscious conduct can be very very effective.

To disregard is not to avoid. In fact, Carl should walk right up to Henry and stand there in his presence. No verbal response would be offered. The object would be to demonstrate to Henry that his conduct does not intimidate.

If Henry persists with his race-conscious offerings, provided his conduct does not become even more offensive, Carl would simply move on without further involvement.

(Henry, "You know, I said that because blacks still have to deal with a lot of discrimination." Carl, "I'm gonna go over this way." Carl moves away and looks at a painting on the wall, or occupies himself in some other manner, perhaps in conversation with other members of the group.)

By disregarding race-conscious conduct, one can accomplish three very important objectives: non involvement in race-conscious activity, refusal to give race-conscious conduct even the benefit of consideration, and negative reinforcement to the misguided who promote race-conscious acts.

Some race-conscious individuals instigate race-conscious activity specifically as an invitation to others to submit or lend themselves to race-conscious engagement. The disregard of race-conscious conduct would reject that invitation, and would deprive the misguided of the race-conscious involvement.

Of course, all race-conscious conduct cannot be disregarded. Some individuals will refuse to be ignored, and will persist with race-conscious activity, despite efforts to disregard their conduct or direct them to other matters. Also, when asked a specific question, or when thoroughly provoked by insult or degradation, it may inappropriate or undignified to even attempt to disregard the situation. Some instances of race-consciousness must be answered in a direct manner.

The object of direct confrontation should be to swiftly and precisely dispose of the issue at hand, without compromising the attitude that race is unimportant.

(Susan is in a car pool. She is a back seat passenger on her way to work. Four other women are in the car. Opinions are being expressed about teen-age pregnancy. Susan is asked, "As a black, Susan, how do you feel about it?" Susan, "I have my own personal opinion. But when you say, "as a black," I don't get involved in things like that?" Driver, "I don't understand." Susan, "I don't believe in generalizations about people on the basis of race." Driver, "But nobody is saying anything bad." Susan, "I don't believe in it.")

It is important, in direct confrontation, not to get involved in a debate over racial assertions. Racial insult is an implication, insinuation, or direct statement that blacks are less deserving than whites. Racial insult is a lie. It would be an indignity to argue against that lie. As previously stated, the worthiness of blacks is not debatable.

One should respond, in direct confrontation, not to the insult, but to the fact that an insult is made. Confront not the lie, but the liar. The lie itself will dissipate in the wind.

In confronting the liar, and not the lie, the initial response to the race-conscious instigator is crucial because the initial response determines the nature and course of the ensuing confrontation. It is especially important at the outset not to discuss the substance of offending statements.

("You're making generalizations about people on the basis of race. I find that offensive.")

("That comment you've just made is offensive.")

("I consider your comment a personal insult.")

(Racially derogatory treatment by a cashier at a supermarket, by an employee at the Motor Vehicle Department, by an airline attendant at a ticket counter, or by similar people serving the public. The response: "Why are you being discourteous to me? You have bowel movements don't you? And in the end, I have to tell you, you're gonna die and rot like everybody else.")

(In response to derogatory comments about blacks, "In the end, you're gonna

die and rot like everybody else. Why do you say bad things about other people?")

("Why do you call me nigger? You old bean head. You're gonna die and rot like everybody else.")

Confronting the liar, and not the lie, would also preclude counter attacks against whites. Racial assaults, even when in response to other racial assaults, serve not only to debate the worthiness of blacks, but also to promote racial animosity and the general best interest of racism.

Some race-conscious individuals, when confronted, will raise questions themselves as to the truthfulness of their assertions.

("Why is that an insult? I don't consider that an insult. There's truth in what I've said and I don't understand why you're offended. I've said it many times before, to blacks and whites, and nobody else has ever objected. I simply want to know why it's an insult. I feel I'm entitled to know.")

("I've just been insulted. And I'm not about to debate this thing with you. If you truly don't understand why your comment (conduct) is offensive, and if it makes a difference to you, I would simply ask that you take some time and think about it. I think it'll come to you. And if it doesn't, then you ask. But not now.")

(Margaret, "I apologize. I certainly didn't intend to offend anyone. I won't do it again. I just didn't realize it was offensive. And I still don't understand why. I wonder if you can help me." Don, "I know you're sincere in what you're saying. But with this type of thing, I have to say to you take some time and think about it. And I think it'll come to you. And if it doesn't, then you could ask. But first, I believe you owe it to yourself to think about it.")

But race-conscious individuals cannot be allowed to induce the offended into humiliating debate or discussion over racial assertions.

Direct confrontation need not and should not always be open and immediate. Private one-on-one discussion is an option well suited for some situations. For example, individuals who persist with race-conscious activity despite the disregard of their conduct, and who cannot be disregarded altogether because association is necessary at work or at other functions or affairs, can probably be best handled when approached in private sessions.

("May I speak with you privately? At your convenience. But it is an important matter.")

Open discussion could cause offending individuals some concern about being portrayed in an unfavorable light among friends or acquaintances. Uneasiness and posturing in the presence of others could preclude the sincere expression of feelings and ideas, and could in fact result in avoidable hostile confrontations. The proper motivation is to frankly explore the problem presented and not to embarrass or to publicly chastise.

Some race-conscious offenders, when confronted, will become unruly beyond what is acceptable as civil behavior. As to this type of situation, no specific suggestions are being offered. One may choose, if permitted by the circumstances, to just walk away from the encounter. On the other hand, one may choose to stay. The offended individual should be guided in this type of situation by his or her own best judgment and personal integrity. The attitude that race is unimportant, however, still must not be compromised.

Blacks who make the commitment to keep matters of race out of their lives will certainly be challenged. And in some cases the challenge presented will be by design.

("Congratulations on your promotion. You're now one of those black managers.")

To some, the idea of blacks behaving as though they are equal in all respects to whites is very disturbing.

Malicious race-conscious conduct especially must be withstood. The above-mentioned "black managers" comment could probably be disregarded. Consider, however, how an employee who believes in the ideas and principles expressed here would respond to disparate treatment by a racially motivated supervisor.

(A supervisor envisions extra work, unfavorable work assignments and even the denial of advancement for an employee in her unit. Supervisor's attitude toward the employee, "What is she doing acting as though race is unimportant? She'll have to recognize race now. She'll have to claim racial discrimination. But that's something she can't prove. She can't prove it.")

The above-mentioned employee under the supervision of the malicious supervisor is in a very difficult situation. But her situation is not impossible. She has the protection of our laws. She can also complain to her personnel department or to individuals in management positions superior to the supervisor. But she ought not to be intimidated by the situation, and should seek first to resolve the matter with the supervisor.

The employee would not necessarily confront each and every incident. She would avoid the trivial. She would not give the supervisor a basis to diminish or belittle her claims. She would confront only those significant incidents wherein the inequity is clearly demonstrable.

Also, the employee should not submit to discussions about racial issues in general. That type of submission would merely accommodate the supervisor who is motivated to focus any and all confrontations on the issue of race. The supervisor wants the employee to debate the worthiness of blacks. Thus, each incident should be confronted separately, as it occurs, and on its own particular facts. Additionally, so as to avoid posturing in the presence of others, confrontation with the supervisor should be on the basis of private one-on-one discussions.

In refusing to debate the worthiness of blacks, the employee should be guided also by the persuasion that victims of racial discrimination should seek relief or remedies, not on the basis that blacks are entitled to certain rights or privileges, but on the basis simply that people are so entitled. An individual denied a job promotion on account of race, for example, should seek a remedy on the grounds alone that he or she is entitled to the position. After all, in cases of discrimination, race is an issue only because the perpetrators make it an issue.

(Employee, "That work assignment is unfair." Supervisor, "How can you say it's unfair? Other employees do it. And nobody has ever complained." Employee, "It's unfair because I've done it five times this month. Nobody else has done it more than once." Supervisor, "Well, it just happened that way. I can't sit around and count every little thing everybody does." Employee, "I don't expect that. I'm talking about fairness. And I think you know the difference." Supervisor, "Are you saying you're being discriminated against because you're black?" Employee, "Now, where did you get that?" Supervisor, "From what you're saying." Employee, "Did I mention race?" Supervisor, "No, but from what you're saying, I assumed that's what you meant." Employee, "I expect to be treated fairly. Insofar as I'm concerned, race has nothing to do with it. It may be a problem for you, but not for me.")

Misguided individuals, who interject race into non racial matters and engage also in malicious race-conscious conduct, in an attempt specifically to compromise blacks in the attitude that they are equal in all respects to whites, cannot be allowed to prevail.

CHAPTER 7

ASSIMILATION

Racial inequities today are everywhere. And yet no one is responsible. Racially discriminatory conduct cannot be isolated from acceptable customs and practices, and thus cannot be destroyed. Misguided people shield racist deeds by attributing their actions to motivations other than race. Motives of ill will are disguised as other legitimate objectives.

The current approach to our racial problem is totally ineffective for the situation presented. Racial discrimination cannot be defeated when fought on its own terms. It must be attacked at its source, at the level of race-consciousness. The elimination of race-consciousness is not just the best way to resolve our racial problem, it is in fact the only way.

We already know all we need to know about the evils of race-consciousness. We experimented with the "separate but equal" doctrine in the United States, with constitutional approval, from 1896 to 1954. Segregated schools and segregated public accommodations were required by law. We have experimented continuously since the events of the 1960's with separate black development. Segregation of the races continues.

Today's separate black development is just as detrimental in many respects as past forced segregation. We have in both cases the separation of blacks from the rest of our society. Racial separation that occurs voluntarily, in attitudes and in the existence of black organizations and affiliations, is not harmless. If segregated schools do indeed deny equal educational opportunities to blacks, then equal opportunity in education is denied when blacks enter into integrated schools and organize at those schools unto themselves into black student organizations. Also, of what benefit is an integrated profession if blacks who enter that profession organize unto themselves for social, educational, and professional activities?

In the 1954 case of Brown v Board of Education, the United States

Supreme Court expressed the view that the association of blacks with others is an important aspect of the educational process. Association in professions, trades, and in other aspects of our society is equally as important. One's association with others determines professional and individual development for many many years after the formal education process ends. Also, people who make important decisions that affect our lives are inclined to award jobs, promotions and other benefits to those individuals in whom they have the most confidence. And, as a practical matter, people are likely to have more confidence in the individuals with whom they associate than in those with whom there is little or no association.

Open and free association, which is crucial for blacks and others as well, is precluded not only when segregation is required by law, but also when blacks segregate voluntarily unto themselves. Separate black development is a continuation of that same old terribly misguided "separate but equal" doctrine. "Separate but equal" is a dangerous concept with which we cannot afford to continue to experiment.

Greatly diminished race-consciousness in the United States as a solution to the racial problem is attainable. Many improvements in our race relations can be accomplished immediately. Other improvements will take time. It takes time to erase harmful racial attitudes. And, unfortunately, some people will not be persuaded at all to abandon their racial prejudices. But, in the long term, that is not a problem. People do expire. The hope and concern is that the recommendations being made here will result in the death of race- consciousness also, and that race-consciousness will not be passed to succeeding generations.

The discontinuance of the practice of race-consciousness would result in the assimilation of blacks into mainstream American life. Assimilation would be accomplished, not compelling people to commingle, but by simply removing the obstacles that prevent or discourage the development of relationships across racial lines. The removal of these obstacles would not interfere with the development of personal relationships between blacks and other blacks, between whites and other whites, or between blacks and whites. There would be no interference in our personal, social or professional affairs. Quite the contrary would be the case. Racial integration, freedom of association, and equal opportunity for all are the laws and policies of our land. And these important objectives would in fact be the realities of our land were it not for contrived race-conscious obstructions. These obstructions must be removed. Assimilation would then occur naturally under the weight of true adherence to our laws and values.

An assimilated United States of America would certainly be a changed United States of America, but the change would be for the better and without question in the best interest of our people and our country.

Assimilation would be relatively painless. And there is truly nothing to fear. We need only put our faith in our Constitution, laws and values. A country committed to the principle of righteousness and justice ought not to be afraid to do the right thing.

Assimilation would require that blacks become involved in new professional, social and personal relationships. Problems encountered in developing these new relationships would be diminished by our overall efforts against race-consciousness. Of course, there would still be some difficulty. But difficulty in our race relations for blacks is not a new experience. Problems in meeting the challenges presented by assimilation certainly would not be any greater than the difficulty blacks are already facing in their daily lives.

To reach out to get involved in new relationships would not be a concession. In fact, it would be a demand. It would be a claim by blacks to all the privileges and opportunities enjoyed by others. Those opportunities being denied must be claimed before equality of treatment can become a reality. All that America has to offer belongs to blacks as much as it does to others. To reach out is not at all an indignity. It is a bold step. It is strength. It is courage. It is confidence.

Of course, some blacks opposed to assimilation wish to distinguish themselves, as a matter of principle, from the country considered responsible for many great wrongs against black citizens. Remaining separate as black Americans allows that distinction. But the realities of our situation are such that black separatism benefits the cause of racism. It would be ironic and indeed tragic if blacks insisted on keeping in place the very object that denies them equal access to the fruits of our society.

Assimilation would not require that blacks deny their skin color. Blacks would simply say by their attitudes and action that race is unimportant. Compromises need not be made. There would be no obligation to accept those things in American life found objectionable. Changes can be made. Worthy values and practices embraced by blacks would not be abandoned, but would be brought forth and introduced to others.

Clear and unequivocal testimony as to the effectiveness of assimilation in resolving matters of discrimination is the American experience with the disparate treatment of European immigrants. European immigrants faced vicious discrimination in the United States on the basis of religion and national origin. That problem has now been greatly diminished, and for many, altogether resolved by the assimilation of European immigrants and their descendants into mainstream American life.

Of course, blacks have been denied assimilation by racist laws and racist practices. Our laws and attitudes are such today, however, that assimilation can be accomplished. Race-consciousness is certainly an obstinate and very intimidating obstruction, but it can be brought down.

CHAPTER 8

POVERTY

It was previously indicated that the high rate of poverty today among blacks is also a racial inequity. The point was made that blacks were forced into poverty, a condition from which there is no escape, by past racist laws and practices. Thus, the racial problem in the United States cannot be completely resolved without addressing the matter of poverty.

Diminished race-consciousness alone would not uplift blacks from poverty. It is essential, nevertheless, in improving the conditions of the poor, to remove race-conscious barriers between black and white citizens. The black and white poor have not demonstrated the capacity to separately resolve their problems. Sadly, they have been prevented by race-consciousness from coming together for that purpose. Political influence and/or public sentiment, of a magnitude sufficient to mobilize America against poverty, cannot be generated by the poor so long as they remain divided along racial lines.

Race-consciousness is an impediment to efforts to eliminate poverty also in that it contributes to a lack of sympathy for impoverished American citizens. Race-consciousness has convinced some people that poverty is essentially a black problem about which they ought not to be concerned.

Additionally, poor whites in the United States have adopted the mistaken belief that they have little or nothing in common with poor blacks. But many barriers in our society that deny opportunities to poor blacks also deny opportunities to poor whites. The cost of housing, which excludes poor blacks from certain neighborhoods, excludes poor whites as well. The cost of education and poor educational backgrounds that exclude poor blacks from colleges, universities and other institutions of higher learning also exclude poor whites. High unemployment, low wages, and the condition of poverty in general, which discourage and destroy ambitions, adversely affect blacks and whites.

The practice of race-consciousness is of no benefit to poor whites. Actually, it keeps them more securely attached in their position. The little barefooted white boy, whether in the rural south or on the streets of Boston, does not serve his cause when he shouts racial insults to blacks. He has been deceived. Not only is his condition of poverty tragic, but he has been taught to work ignorantly against his own best interest.

Race-consciousness divides. It misdirects. It diffuses. It misplaces efforts that otherwise could be used to uplift the poor from their condition. Poor whites and poor blacks do not join together as they should. Instead, they blame each other for their misfortunes. They turn to each other and hate. They hate. They resent. They mistrust. And poverty goes on.

It is essential that race-consciousness now be relieved of its role as a dominant factor in the maintenance of poverty. Efforts to uplift the poor on a race-conscious basis must be abandoned. Measures to help the black poor only are in reality self defeating (although short term benefits may be derived). Race-conscious efforts promote race-consciousness to the detriment of all of us. Accordingly, and because it is the right thing to do morally, we must strive to uplift all poor people in our country, without regard to race, color, religion or national origin.

The current approach to poverty gives great attention to the immediate needs of the poor. And it is certainly important that we adequately address these needs. We must continue and indeed improve our efforts in this regard. But attention to the immediate needs of the poor is not a solution to the problem of poverty. We must ultimately place the poor in a position sufficient for them to obtain on their own benefits and opportunities available to the general population. Thus, we will arrive at a true solution to poverty, not when the poor are adequately cared for, but when the poor are uplifted altogether from their condition, and are no longer impoverished.

It was stated previously that the poor are precluded by the very conditions in which they live from doing the things necessary to improve their lives. They are distracted by the anxieties of crime, deteriorated housing, low income and family instability. They are preoccupied with immediate needs and desires and cannot sustain long term courses of action necessary to uplift them from their condition. Frustration, hopelessness and despair dominant their lives. Meaningful ambitions and aspirations do not develop.

In resolving the problem of poverty, we must look to education. Education is a dominant consideration in our society in awarding jobs and many other opportunities. Education provides knowledge of how one must proceed to accomplish certain goals. It provides knowledge as to how one must manage his or her affairs in general to be successful. It raises the level of expectation. It enhances self esteem. It instills confidence and gives direction. It serves as a focus and thus gives individuals the strength and the desire to avoid drugs, teenage pregnancies, criminal conduct and other maladies that affect the poor disproportionately. Focus on education gives individuals the capacity to withstand domination by harmful environmental circumstances.

Education has the capacity to truly break the vicious cycle of poverty. It will break that cycle, however, only if it is made readily accessible to the poor, and only if the poor can be motivated to pursue it, notwithstanding the disabling detriments of the conditions in which they live.

Making education accessible would require that we enhance efforts already being made to provide scholarships, student loans, grants and work-study programs to those individuals in need. We must put the poor in a position financially to attend our colleges, universities, trade schools and other institutions of higher learning. We must also ensure that the education provided to the poor at all levels equals that provided to others.

Equality of education for blacks is believed by some to depend on our ability to integrate our schools. Inequality in facilities, supplies, student to teacher ratio and the like is usually found in cases of school segregation. Unfortunately, school integration is a goal we have not been able to achieve.

School segregation is due largely to the fact that we have racially segregated neighborhoods. Students typically attend schools within their own communities. The widespread bussing of students out of their communities for the purpose of overall school integration would be an awesome burden to place on our children. It is also an idea that the American people are apparently not willing to accept. Thus, school integration without total assimilation of blacks into mainstream American life probably cannot be accomplished.

Also, school integration alone would not be a complete answer to our problem. The state maintenance of segregated schools does indeed result in unequal education opportunities. But integrated schools do not necessarily result in equality. School integration does not address the problems of low level expectation and student motivation.

Integrated school situations do not preclude the harmful perception that blacks and the poor lack the capacity to perform at the same level as others. Blacks and the poor are denied equality in education in that they are not expected to perform well academically. Consequently, the effort is not made to prepare them beyond low level expectations.

We cannot afford to let unfortunate misconceptions determine the level at which our students perform. It is incumbent upon us to set proper student standards and to insist that our standards be met. Poor quality in student performance simply must be rejected.

The ultimate solution to low level student expectation would be the elimination of erroneous attitudes and perceptions. Much can be done in this regard by diminishing our reliance on race-consciousness in the ways already recommended. Other corrective action should involve specific measures to set and maintain high academic standards.

Desired standards of student performance can be established by requiring our young people, in elementary schools and high schools, to pass tests in reading, writing, math and achievement before being promoted from one grade level to the next. This recommended test requirement would be in addition to other school requirements and would not preclude or replace other methods of evaluating student performance.

It is imperative that students be tested at each grade level. It would be a mistake, for example, to test on a one time basis at or near the time of high school graduation. The time of graduation is much too late to tell students what is expected of them. Also, tests should be administered and graded by individuals or entities outside the various schools. Testing and grading by the schools themselves could result in each school adopting its own separate standards. It is important to maintain uniformity of student standards throughout each school district (indeed throughout the country).

Multiple test sessions for each grade level would be held during each school year. Students would have options as to when to submit for examination. They would have the opportunity as well, in the event of test failure, to test a second and perhaps even a third time during the school term. Test sessions could also be held during summer months.

It would be necessary, as a matter of fairness, to gradually phase in these testing procedures. An abrupt implementation would likely result in hardships to some students, especially those at the higher grade levels. Students should be given a reasonable length of time to adjust to new demands.

Special incentives would be used as additional motivation for teachers to prepare their students to satisfy test requirements. Programs that publicly recognize and reward successful teaching efforts would be promoted. For example, a math teacher would be publicly recognized if the students in his or her class perform well on the math portion of a given test. Teacher recognition would serve also in the interest of accountability in that unsuccessful teaching efforts would not be rewarded.

The tests being recommended here, and indeed the general academic programs at our schools, would emphasize proficiency in the basics. Proficiency in math and reading and writing is essential to quality in education. Examinations at each grade level would strenuously test our students in these areas.

The general academic programs at our schools would continue with the requirement that students take certain basic courses. Schools would also implement a required a course at each grade level specifically in reading and writing. Our students would be taught to understand, explain, interpret, and discuss the implications of what they read. They would be taught to express ideas, thoughts, arguments, and opinions in writing. They would be required to do various writing assignments.

In providing equality of education, student motivation is equally as important as maintaining high academic standards. Vigorous academic programs alone would not sufficiently improve student performance. A student who attends a quality school during the day and returns at the end of each day to the condition of poverty is still at a tremendous disadvantage.

Efforts to motivate the poor to pursue education should be directed at entire communities and not solely at students. Students are influenced tremendously by the attitudes and values of the people who surround them. Community attitudes and values, which do not have a sufficiently high regard for education, may operate so as to neutralize narrow attempts to reach students only. It would be extremely difficult, if not altogether impossible, to sufficiently motivate students without also motivating other members of our communities. Moreover, working people and the unemployed should be mobilized to improve their lives as well. Some individuals can be persuaded to return to the pursuit of education.

Providing motivation to pursue education is essentially a matter of building confidence. The poor people of our country, adults and children, have little or no confidence today in education. The assertion that education leads to specific jobs and occupations is, to them, a vague and uncertain proposition. Also, the poor are just not convinced that opportunities actually exist for them to become engaged in meaningful courses of study. Thus, it is important to persuade the poor not only that education works but also that it can and will work for the impoverished.

Confidence in education is derived from knowledge. It arises out of an understanding of how our system operates. An explicit understanding is necessary. Vague notions or the mere statement that education is good for you is not sufficient. People believe education will improve their lives, not simply because someone says it will, but because they have a clear and precise understanding of how it will do so.

The specific knowledge that gives confidence in education is not provided at our schools. It is acquired by the fortunate essentially through association. Parents, friends and others convey meaningful information on the opportunities, operation, and peculiarities of our system. Association, of course, is of little or no benefit in this regard to the poor. The poor associate primarily with the poor. Vital information is not available among them in the first instance to be passed from one to the other.

It will be necessary, in addressing the problem presented, to make special efforts to expose the poor to that information that gives confidence in education. It will be necessary to expose the poor to specific information, not only on jobs, occupations and professions in our society, but also on what course of action one must take to succeed. The poor people of our country must be exposed to information that will enable them, notwithstanding the detriments of poverty, to focus their lives on positive uplifting ambitions.

Vital information can be provided to the poor by the operation and maintenance of Personal Development Centers in selected communities throughout the country. The organizational structure of these Centers would consist of boards of directors, bylaws, executive directors, and members. Membership would be on the basis of households. One household would constitute one member. All individuals of each member household would be eligible and encouraged to participate in Center programs.

Each Personal Development Center would have an auditorium or assembly room for the presentation of weekly lessons to community residents. Centers with active community participation unable to assemble all participating residents in a single sitting would use multiple sessions. For example, households A through K could be designated to attend the weekly session on Wednesday nights, with households L through Z attending the weekly session on Saturday mornings.

Weekly lessons would be open to all community residents, without regard to age or educational background. Working people, elementary school students, high school students, the retired, the unemployed and others would attend. Lessons would be held on weekends and during evening hours on weekdays. Evening and weekend hours would accommodate the schedules of working people and full time students.

Lessons at Personal Development Centers would explore specific jobs, occupations, professions, colleges, universities, trade schools, financial aid programs, and other pertinent subjects and topics. Presentations too lengthy to be completed in one session would be continued to the following week. And lessons would be designed, to the extent possible, to reach adults and children, and all people attending, without regard to academic background.

Lessons at Personal Development Centers would provide community residents with specific information on what is involved in the various jobs, occupations, and careers in our country. Matters such as pay, working conditions, work locations, prestige and the like would be fully explored. Specific information would be provided on what education, training and other courses of action individuals would have to pursue to enter into certain areas.

There would be lessons also on how to successfully proceed in the pursuit of higher education. Centers would provide information on admission requirements, quality and kind of education, tradition, prestige, student life, and other matters involving specific colleges, universities, and other institutions of higher learning. Opportunities for financial aid would be explored.

Instruction would be provided on matters of personal management as well. Instruction in personal management would eliminate many problems among the poor due to bad personal decisions. The poor frequently get themselves into bad situations or fail to take advantage of opportunities because they do not have sufficient information upon which to make informed decisions.

Personal management lessons would cover matters such as consumer loans, home mortgages, credit cards, savings accounts, interest rates, legal rights, auto and life insurance, the operation of local, state and federal governments and other similar topics. Informed individuals with personal management skills would be put in a position to intelligently direct the course of their lives.

Instruction in personal management would be augmented by periodic sessions on current events. Local, national and world issues would be analyzed and discussed. Communities would be kept informed of the important social, economic, and political matters affecting their lives.

Weekly lessons at Personal Development Centers would be taught by individuals employed or engaged in various jobs, trades, professions, and occupations. Instructors would instruct in their respective areas of expertise. A bank manager, for example, would present a lesson on jobs in the banking industry. An electrician would instruct on what electricians do. A college administrator would lecture on the process involved in getting a college education.

Each instructor would tell community residents, during the presentation of his or her lesson, precisely what one must do to enter into the field or area discussed. Each instructor would also give a brief description of how he or she personally entered into that particular field or area, and elevated to his or her current level or position.

Also, a brief social occasion, with perhaps a few snacks or refreshments, would be held at the Centers immediately following each weekly session. Instructors would attend, each following his or her own presentation, and associate and commingle with community residents.

People from various jobs, trades and professions, who deliver lessons at Personal Development Centers, share information about their own personal success, and participate in social occasions, would not only disseminate vital information, but would also serve as positive role models for community residents. Residents would associate and identify with instructors and come to believe that they too can achieve and succeed.

It would be necessary to persuade community residents to get involved in and stay with the programs offered by Personal Development Centers. Participation in the programs would be promoted as the good, decent, and proper thing to do. Personal interviews, telephone communications, mailings, public gatherings and other instruments would be used to convey the message that it is extremely important to expose the community to that essential information that enables individuals to progress and succeed in life.

Promotional campaigns would emphasize the importance of participation by adults and children, and even by individuals who personally do not expect to advance in their occupations. The point would be made that attendance at weekly lessons would provide residents with information, without regard to their own personal advancement, sufficient for them to encourage and reinforce the aspirations of others. The point would be made that parents especially would be provided with information to positively influence the lives of their children.

Community interest and participation would be further enhanced by programs of academic competition, with attractive awards and prizes for the contestants. Awards and prizes would consist of cash, goods, services, certificates and public recognition.

Competition at various age and academic levels in math, reading, writing, and achievement, and even on subjects covered in weekly lessons would be held. Only individuals regularly attending weekly lessons and actively participating in Center programs would be allowed to compete. Each contestant would compete at his or her own level. And there would be awards and prizes for each contest.

The academic contests would culminate periodically in tournaments involving top contestants. Award and prizes would go to individuals who qualify for the tournaments. Top awards and prizes would be reserved for tournament winners.

At least one preparation session would be held for each scheduled competition, for the age or academic level involved. Participants would be provided at preparation sessions with rules and procedures on upcoming contests, and would be given direction on how to prepare themselves academically for the events. Participants would be told what subjects or matters to study. They would be directed to books and other sources. Some source material, if available, would be handed out or loaned to them. Practice exercises would be suggested. Individuals would also be directed to adult education courses and other educational programs open to the public.

Additionally, individuals preparing for academic contests would be organized into study groups. Study groups would be assisted and directed by tutors. At least one tutor would be assigned to each group.

Each study group would separately determine the time, place and frequency of its meetings.

Academic competition sponsored by Personal Development Centers would serve, not only to enhance community participation in Center programs, but also to directly influence the poor to focus on education and regard education as a very important part of their lives. Academic preparation for competition would serve further to improve community residents in reading, writing and achievement, and thus put them in a more favorable position to qualify for job placement, job training, and job promotion. Also, the poor would become more competent, capable and knowledgeable in general. Competence would give residents the confidence to reach out in the world and take full advantage of available opportunities.

Community participation in Center programs would be enhanced also by community participation itself. A sense of involvement and togetherness would be derived from participation in the programs offered. A sense of involvement and togetherness would be derived from participation on committees and boards of directors charged with carrying out Center operations.

Parenthetically, involvement and togetherness would benefit the poor even beyond matters of participation enhancement. Involvement and togetherness would actually help the poor withstand the conditions of poverty. In this regard, specific efforts should be made to bring people together to share information and concerns. Meetings, social gatherings and other events would be used to create and maintain a sense of community. There would be a sharing of information on how to solve problems. Residents would be motivated to aid and assist each other. Involvement and togetherness would provide positive reinforcement, moral support, and inspiration.

In addition to providing weekly lessons and academic competition, Personal Development Centers would initiate and maintain programs to reward and publicly recognize community residents who excel in education. Public officials and other respected individuals would be asked to participate in award ceremonies.

Efforts would be made to firmly and permanently establish education as a primary and focal consideration in the lives of community residents. Centers would attempt to maintain a consciousness that education is to be highly regarded and vigorously pursued. The view that education is of great importance would be constantly reinforced.

Personal Development Centers would also assist and direct students in selecting appropriate schools and making applications for school admission. Assistance would be provided as well in placing individuals in jobs and training programs. Individuals out of school with a desire to return to education would be directed to the appropriate programs and institutions.

In the interest of communication, Personal Development Centers would publish and distribute a monthly, bi-weekly or weekly newsletter. The newsletter would keep residents informed of events and activities, awards and prizes, and other important matters affecting their lives.

Personal Development Centers would be established and assisted in selected communities throughout the United States by sponsors. Each Center would be sponsored by one, or more than one, resourceful individual, group, association, business, church or civil organization.

Sponsors of Personal Development Centers would organize the Centers, recruit households into membership, retain the right to participate in Center operations, and actually participate continuously on boards of directors and in management matters in general. Sponsors would work with community residents and the management of the Centers 1) to recruit volunteers to instruct weekly lessons, 2) to recruit tutors for study groups, 3) to administer and manage academic competition, 4) to solicit individuals, businesses and others to donate awards and prizes for academic competition, 5) to conduct award ceremonies, and 6) to raise funds for Center operations. Also, sponsors would make financial contributions to the Centers, if in a position to do so, but direct financial support would not necessarily be a major responsibility.

The cost of operating and maintaining Personal Development Centers would not be prohibitive. As indicated, Centers would rely heavily on volunteers. Of course, some financial support would be necessary. Centers would probably have to seek some financial assistance from businesses, private foundations, and governmental agencies. In the interest of establishing a reliable and predictable source of income, however, an effort should be made to rely as heavily as possible on the people whose lives are immediately involved.

Member households would be required to pay a moderate weekly or monthly membership fee. Each household would be assessed on the basis of the number of people in the household. The greater the number the larger the fee. No one, however, would be denied access to the Centers for inability to pay. In special situations, dues would be modified or waived.

Also, various fund-raising activities such as dinners, dances, talent shows, the sale of baked goods, and the like, would be held in the communities by community residents.

Part Three:
Debate of the Issues

CHAPTER 9

DEBATE OF THE ISSUES

INQUIRER: If I understand you correctly, there are, in your opinion, basically two racial inequities.

AUTHOR: Yes.

INQUIRER: Race-consciousness and poverty.

AUTHOR: That's correct.

INQUIRER: It's interesting to me that you have not described the problem in terms of racism.

AUTHOR: Of course, I did use the term.

INQUIRER: But you don't see racism as being the problem.

AUTHOR: Racism is not a functional definition. It's a restriction, in my opinion. You have to look beyond conduct we recognize as racist. And I think I've been very clear on the reasons why.

INQUIRER: And your solution to the problem, the overall racial problem, is to get out of the business of race-consciousness?

AUTHOR: That's part of it.

INQUIRER: And, of course, to uplift people from poverty?

AUTHOR: Yes.

INQUIRER: And that's your solution.

AUTHOR: I think that's the approach we should take.

INQUIRER: It's a solution?

AUTHOR: Yes, it's a solution.

INQUIRER: That simple?

AUTHOR: I didn't say it was simple.

INQUIRER: I mean, what's complicated about it? You get rid of race-consciousness and you get people out of poverty. What could be so complicated about that?

AUTHOR: If you're suggesting by your comment that I don't understand the difficulty of our racial situation, I have to tell you you're mistaken.

INQUIRER: I'm not suggesting anything?

AUTHOR: I think you are.

INQUIRER: I'm asking a basic question. What's so complicated about eliminating race-consciousness and uplifting people from poverty?

AUTHOR: I discussed those complications.

INQUIRER: I don't think you understand those complications.

AUTHOR: That's your opinion.

INQUIRER: Do you realize we have some outstanding black people in America dedicating their lives to rid this country of racism?

AUTHOR: I've said as much.

INQUIRER: And these people, many of them, are highly educated and well respected by both blacks and whites. And they have lived with the issues and have proven to people what they are capable of doing.

AUTHOR: I agree with you.

INQUIRER: And what you're saying is that these people don't know what they're doing?

AUTHOR: I've said our current approach to the problem is wrong.

INQUIRER: You're saying they don't know what they're doing.

AUTHOR: That's not what I'm saying.

INQUIRER: But that's the implication.

AUTHOR: That's not the implication.

INQUIRER: You're saying they don't know what they're doing. That's what you're saying. And I say to you, just who in the hell do you think you are?!

AUTHOR: I know who I am, believe me.

INQUIRER: You're a nobody. Don't you agree with that?

AUTHOR: I don't agree with that.

INQUIRER: In terms of leadership, and I'll even use the term "black" leadership, and I know you don't like it. In terms of black leadership, can you seriously maintain that you have any credentials whatsoever?

AUTHOR: Let me just respond to these things you're saying one at a time.

INQUIRER: I expect you to respond.

AUTHOR: You're implying that I'm showing a discourtesy or a lack of respect for black people today in positions of leadership. Now, that's just not the case. You are assuming, in the first place, that blacks are not going to agree with me. And that is a big big assumption on your part.

INQUIRER: You really think they're going to agree with you?

AUTHOR: You have assumed that they won't. And I don't think you can make that assumption. You know, you would make it appear as though I'm alone in the ideas and beliefs I have expressed.

INQUIRER: What can you offer to show that you're not alone?

AUTHOR: Impressions and feelings I get from my association with people. And let me tell you also that the ideas I have expressed are not an affront to anybody or anything except race-consciousness. The ideas I have expressed are not to disparage those efforts people are making today against racial inequities. What I am saying is this: let's continue with our fight against racial inequities. But let us now take a different route to get us where we want to go. We all want the same thing. We all want equality of treatment. In my opinion, and I believe it very deeply, separate black development can't take us there.

INQUIRER: And you can?

AUTHOR: I can't, but the approach I'm recommending certainly can.

INQUIRER: Ever seem strange to you that the people out there on the front line against racism never came up with the ideas you're suggesting? Ever occur to you that your ideas are unworkable and totally without merit, and that's why they have never surfaced?

AUTHOR: But they have surfaced. And they didn't before now perhaps because separate black development had to run its course. I don't know.

INQUIRER: That's what you say.

AUTHOR: Then let me say this, also. Your very premise that these ideas will be rejected simply because they are critical of black separatism does not give much credit to blacks in positions of leadership. Any leader, worth anything at all, who truly believes in equality of treatment, and who is truly convinced by these ideas, is not going to insist on separate black development. Leaders who truly believe they have been wrong on the issues will say so. Because they realize that the paramount object, in these matters of race, is not to prove a position correct, but to improve the quality of life for millions of people in the United States who have been denied opportunities. Ego is not the issue. And ego will not prevail. In an opportunist, perhaps. But not in true leaders. And, in any case, as I've just said, the ideas I have expressed are not to challenge the cause against racial inequities, but to continue that cause on a changed course of direction.

INQUIRER: You spoke about my premise. Now, how about yours, that only people concerned about their egos would disagree with you?

AUTHOR: That's not what I've said.

INQUIRER: Well, that's the impression one would get.

AUTHOR: I was merely responding to a very narrow point you raised. No, I realize there can be disagreement with me on the issues. And that I can respect. But to dismiss these ideas on the basis of some predisposition, without even reaching the issues, would be despicable, in my opinion.

INQUIRER: You're not directing that at me?

AUTHOR: I don't have anybody in mind in particular.

INQUIRER: Your ideas and recommendations don't intimidate me.
AUTHOR: I never had that impression.
INQUIRER: At this time, I'd like to take up the ideas themselves. There's one basic criticism I want to make. And I'll make that criticism. Of course, I don't have any expectation whatsoever that I'll be able to change your mind.
AUTHOR: Perhaps, I can change yours.
INQUIRER: You don't really believe that.
AUTHOR: I'm going to try. Let me hear your criticism. And I'll do my best to respond to it in a fair and accurate manner. But before we go on, I just want to answer one other previous thing you said. I don't want to go on without answering.
INQUIRER: All right.
AUTHOR: You said I don't have credentials as a black leader.
INQUIRER: Am I wrong about that?
AUTHOR: Without restating my position on what's wrong with being perceived as a black leader, let me just say to you that I am not trying to sell myself. I'm promoting ideas. And the ideas I'm promoting are independent of me. These ideas have a power and an energy of their own. And my credentials, whatever they are, are ultimately not the issue.
INQUIRER: You can't believe that.
AUTHOR: These ideas, ultimately, I promise you, will carry themselves.
INQUIRER: I'd like to invite you to the real world. In considering ideas and opinions, and in determining what weight to give to those ideas and opinions, in the real world, people consider the source. And that's a reality, my friend. A reality you simply cannot ignore.
AUTHOR: Ultimately these ideas will carry themselves.
INQUIRER: You are the source. And that makes you an issue.
AUTHOR: To that extent, yes. But only to that extent. In terms of presenting the ideas and getting people to consider them fairly, I am an issue. I understand that. Now, I certainly want and seek all the help I can get in promoting what I believe to be right. But I don't agree that these ideas have to be introduced by someone of certain national stature, or anything like that. Ultimately, these ideas will carry themselves. And that's the way it should be.
INQUIRER: So, what do we have here? Do you deny you are an issue, or what?
AUTHOR: To the extent I've just said, I am an issue.
INQUIRER: I would assume then, since you are an issue, to whatever extent, that you'd be willing to submit your qualifications.
AUTHOR: I'll give you information about my background, if that's what you mean. And that's not something I would hesitate to do.

INQUIRER: I'll begin by asking you what is your occupation.
AUTHOR: Attorney.
INQUIRER: Are you a lawyer?
AUTHOR: I am.
INQUIRER: What type of law do you practice?
AUTHOR: I defend people in accident cases.
INQUIRER: You're a defense lawyer?
AUTHOR: Yes.
INQUIRER: How long have you been a lawyer?
AUTHOR: Fourteen years.
INQUIRER: Are you involved in politics?
AUTHOR: I vote, and I have political opinions.
INQUIRER: I'm speaking of something beyond that. For example, are you involved in any political organizations? Do you actively support political candidates? Are you a political adviser? Are you involved in anything like that?
AUTHOR: No.
INQUIRER: Have you ever been involved in politics, in the sense I've just described?
AUTHOR: Sixteen or seventeen years ago, I was involved very briefly in a contest for state representative. I didn't get the endorsement I was seeking and that was the end of it.
INQUIRER: Were you involved at all during the 1960's in the protest activities of the Civil Rights Movement?
AUTHOR: No.
INQUIRER: That wasn't before your time, was it? I know you've cautioned me about making assumptions.
AUTHOR: In December of 1964, I turned eighteen. And at that time, just to give you a little more information, I enlisted into the Air Force. My first permanent assignment was Blytheville, Arkansas. And I stayed there for about twelve months. In the summer of 1966, I was transferred to Spain. And I was in Spain until I got out of the service in December of 1968.
INQUIRER: So, I guess what you're saying is that, during a good portion of the Civil Rights Movement, you were away in military service.
AUTHOR: Yes.
INQUIRER: And, in fact, for at least two and a half years, you were even out of the country?
AUTHOR: As I've just said.
INQUIRER: Are you also saying that had you not been away in the service, that you would have been involved in protest activities of the Civil Rights Movement?
AUTHOR: I am not saying that. And I can't say that. When I was

eighteen, I didn't even know what a protest activity was. There's just no way to know how I would have developed, or what situations I would have encountered. I just don't know.

INQUIRER: What can you tell me then about your Civil Rights activities after the military service?

AUTHOR: During what period of time?

INQUIRER: Yesterday, the day before, five years ago, anytime since you've been out of the service.

AUTHOR: Well, in 1969 I filed a discrimination complaint against a company where I was working. Is that the type of thing you're talking about?

INQUIRER: If you think it's important.

AUTHOR: Then I should tell you also that during my second year as a law student I filed a complaint against my law school.

Inquirer: Okay.

AUTHOR: In the late 1970's, I attended a demonstration against racism in Washington, D.C. And soon after that, I participated in some activities against the Klu Klux Klan.

INQUIRER: Anything else?

AUTHOR: As I think about it, I believe that's it. Of course, and I know you understand this, I've encountered numerous racial incidents over the years, some subtle and some not so subtle, and I have contended with these incidents, as people do, as I've gone about my life.

INQUIRER: I'm speaking obviously of something beyond your day-to-day handling of those types of incidents.

AUTHOR: And what I've said is all I can tell you about that.

INQUIRER: Perhaps I should ask you a little more about those activities you mentioned. The complaint against that company in 1969, what was that all about?

AUTHOR: I was working there part time as I was attending college. And I found, and I was really amazed by this, that the company still had racially segregated bathrooms and lunchrooms. And blacks were not being allowed to advance on the job. I filed my complaint with the federal Equal Employment Opportunity Commission. There was an investigation and the government agreed with me that the company was violating the law.

INQUIRER: I assume corrective action was taken.

AUTHOR: The segregation was terminated and people I know, some of them my relatives, were upgraded in their jobs.

INQUIRER: You must've have been proud of that accomplishment?

AUTHOR: Actually, I was. This company was a substantial employer. And still is today. It's considered a prestigious place to work. So, it was important.

INQUIRER: Tell me about your complaint against the law school.

AUTHOR: That complaint was filed with the federal Department, at that time, of Health, Education, and Welfare. And as the situation progressed, the black students and the law school reached an agreement that a certain individual from Harvard would come down and investigate. And that individual did come down. I believe he conducted interviews, reviewed records, and I don't know what else. And he submitted a written report. And in that report he complained that there were very few blacks in the legal profession in the state. He complained also about the low number of blacks in law school. But there was no specific finding of racial discrimination.

INQUIRER: So, what happened to your complaint?

AUTHOR: I believe the government concluded, on the basis of that written report, that there was no discrimination, and closed its file.

INQUIRER: What prompted you to file the complaint in the first place?

AUTHOR: I felt the grading of black students was on a discriminatory basis. As I look back today, however, I'm not sure that was the case.

INQUIRER: What happened to change your mind?

AUTHOR: I think I was just responding to the overall situation. The racial atmosphere at the law school at that time was very oppressive. Professors and fellow students had an attitude that blacks didn't belong there. Of course, not all whites felt that way. We had friends. But some whites were downright hostile. It was an intense situation for black students.

INQUIRER: The demonstration in Washington, D.C. and the things you did against the Klan in the late 1970's, how did you become engaged in those activities?

AUTHOR: My wife knew some people who had strong commitments against racism. She introduced me and I got involved.

INQUIRER: Not to belittle what you've done, but in considering your past, I don't think one can say you've really been active in the fight for racial justice.

AUTHOR: And that's not a claim that I'm making. I'm just responding to your questions. You have to understand something. Fighting racial inequities is not for me an occupation or a profession I've decided to pursue. I'd rather be about my own personal aspirations. And that's precisely what I've been doing with my life. I'm involved in trying to resolve the racial problem now, not because I sought it out, but because it's there and because it provokes me.

INQUIRER: And that's the question I want to ask. Why didn't it provoke you before now? It's always been there.

AUTHOR: Of course, I was provoked before now. I don't mean to suggest otherwise. It is difficult to conceive of any black person living in the United States and not being provoked. And I've been involved in activities as I've described.

INQUIRER: But my question is why have you waited until now to get involved as you are today.

AUTHOR: I understood that to be your question. And I was going to respond.

INQUIRER: Please.

AUTHOR: When I got out of the service in 1968, I had some racial apprehensions at that time, certainly, but I truly thought, and perhaps in retrospect it was more a matter of hope than belief, that the racial problem in the United States had been resolved. After all, we finally had laws against racial discrimination. You couldn't do that any more. The racial incidents I encountered I thought were just residuals that would dissipate merely with the passing of time. And so I was about pursuing my own personal aspirations, as I've said. I did realize, of course, in the ensuing years, that the problem had not been resolved. But I didn't feel it was my job to resolve it. Other people were working on it. And all was as well as it could be. As we continued over the years, without an improvement, in my opinion, I started to analyze the whole situation. And I came to the point where I am today.

INQUIRER: And what point is that?

AUTHOR: To firmly believe that the approach I have discussed is the way to finally resolve our racial problems.

INQUIRER: In view of your ideas and opinions on our racial situation, there is a question I think I must ask you. Were you personally helped or aided in any way by race-conscious affirmative action in your education or in your professional development as a lawyer?

AUTHOR: Yes.

INQUIRER: And yet race-conscious affirmative action is something you want to abolish?

AUTHOR: That's correct.

INQUIRER: That's an inconsistency, isn't it? Or is it your view that you've gotten yours, so the heck with everybody else?

AUTHOR: That's not my view. That's not my attitude at all.

INQUIRER: Do you think you would have ever become a lawyer without race-conscious affirmative action?

AUTHOR: I don't know.

INQUIRER: You never would have been admitted to law school.

AUTHOR: Is that a question? Or is that your statement? You're certainly free to say whatever you believe.

INQUIRER: It's a question. Isn't it a fact you never would have been admitted to law school?

AUTHOR: I wouldn't call it a fact. But let me tell you something, you may be correct in what you're saying. I don't know. I don't think, however, that I would have given up very easily. I just can't say what would have happened. Also, as for me personally, you have to understand that it was never my feeling that I had to become a lawyer. With or without law school, with or without race-conscious affirmative action, I would have gone on with my life.

INQUIRER: But with what type of life? That's my question.

AUTHOR: Who knows?

INQUIRER: Are you saying you would have been as prosperous as you are today?

AUTHOR: I don't know. Maybe I would have gone in a different direction. But I'm not going to say I would have failed in my ambitions. Because I don't believe that.

INQUIRER: You think you would have done all right?

AUTHOR: Well, that's what I'm saying.

INQUIRER: What do you say about other blacks?

AUTHOR: Blacks would have managed well without race-conscious affirmative action. That's what I believe.

INQUIRER: And blacks in the past who entered into jobs, professions, occupations and trades with the aid of race-conscious affirmative action would have been able to do so even without it?

AUTHOR: That's not a statement I would make. Some, yes. But if you're saying all blacks, I don't think so.

INQUIRER: And if some blacks, who are now successful, had been denied opportunities, that would have been all right with you.

AUTHOR: In my judgment, as I've said, the promotion of race-consciousness is by far the greater harm. Look, I recognize the fact that good people did benefit from race-conscious affirmative action. I don't dispute that at all. And I don't oppose efforts to help people. But let's go about our business in helping people without race-conscious involvement. Let's work to make more opportunities available in education for all our citizens. Let's implement and maintain programs to help the poor in admission to colleges, trade schools, training programs, professional schools, and universities, without regard to race or skin color.

INQUIRER: I understand what you're proposing.

AUTHOR: I want to say this to you. You know, some people may agree with me that race-consciousness today is bad, and yet believe race-conscious affirmative action was good and necessary for an initial period of time following the Civil Rights Movement.

INQUIRER: But that's not your position?

AUTHOR: Correct. That's not my position. My point is this: I would say to those people, what's done is done. Good or bad, we have had race-conscious affirmative action. Whether it was good or bad in that initial period following the Civil Rights Movement is not something upon which we have to agree. It is sufficient if we can agree, at least as of now, that race-conscious affirmative action and other race-conscious efforts should be abandoned.

INQUIRER: With your permission, I'll move now to that basic criticism I mentioned earlier I wanted to take up with you.

AUTHOR: Okay.

INQUIRER: My criticism is that there is nothing to motivate people to implement what you are proposing. Assume for the moment that you do have good ideas. Many people won't accept that. But assume for the moment that you do. Do you really think people will just come up to you and say, "Gee, those are some great ideas, and we're going to implement 'em just like you say?" I mean, are you really that naive?

AUTHOR: Continuing racial discord. I discussed that. Continuing racial discord is a problem for all of us. That is the motivation.

INQUIRER: But when you tell people racial discord is going to be a problem, they don't believe it. Isn't that so?

AUTHOR: Well, whatever people believe, it is a problem.

INQUIRER: But that's not the point, is it? If the threat of racial discord is going to motivate people, people are going to have to believe it's a problem. I think you have to agree with me on that. Assume that it's a certainty that racial discord will develop, if we don't do something about it, so as to completely destroy this country. Even if the destruction of our country is a certainty, people would still have to believe it's going to happen. If they don't believe it's going to happen, and it happens anyway, then, of course, we'd go down as a Nation with our hands in our pockets. But the point is this: people still would not have been motivated.

AUTHOR: I certainly understand what you're saying.

INQUIRER: So, what's the answer?

AUTHOR: You convince people as to the dangers of our situation. That's what I'm trying to do.

INQUIRER: You think you're going to be successful in that?

AUTHOR: To some degree, I would hope so.

INQUIRER: But your ideas and suggestions depend on it.

AUTHOR: Not entirely.

INQUIRER: They don't?

AUTHOR: No.

INQUIRER: I don't understand.

AUTHOR: I have to tell you that I don't accept your premise that it is naive to expect people to do what is right.

INQUIRER: Do you expect people to implement your ideas just because it would be the right thing to do?

AUTHOR: I do.

INQUIRER: You do?

AUTHOR: I do.

INQUIRER: Then I extend the invitation, once again: come out, come out, from wherever you are, my friend, and join me in the real world.

AUTHOR: The motivation among the American people to do the right thing is a power too good and too awesome to be dismissed.

INQUIRER: Okay, then don't dismiss it. But are you really and truly going to rely on it?

AUTHOR: I do rely on it.

INQUIRER: Listen to me. In the real world, people are motivated by money, politics and other matters of self interest, and not by considerations of morality. You don't like that. But that's just the way it is, my friend. That's just the way it is.

AUTHOR: If this racial problem in the United States is going to be resolved, and I believe in my heart that it will be, then it's going to be resolved, not on the basis of self interest or some black power movement, but on the basis that the American people want to do the right thing.

INQUIRER: What you're talking about is just not there. The motivation to resolve our racial problem on the basis of morality is just not there. I think you know its not there. If it were there, then we wouldn't have a racial problem. Ask yourself this question. You've seen the President of the United States on television campaigning for and against certain issues. For example, you've seen both Presidents Reagan and Bush on t.v. campaigning against drugs. Why is it that you haven't seen a campaign like that against racism? You know why you haven't seen it? You haven't seen it because the motivation is not there. We have the capacity to resolve our racial problem. But the motivation is just not there.

AUTHOR: I agree with you wholeheartedly. The motivation to resolve our racial problem is not there, as you say. But the motivation to do the right thing is there.

INQUIRER: How can you be motivated to do the right thing, and not be motivated to resolve our racial problem? Are you saying people don't know what's right? The right thing to do is to discontinue the racist treatment of blacks in this country. How could anyone with even a hint of human decency not know that?

AUTHOR: But people don't know that. In a vague and general sense, they do. But they don't have a true appreciation of the inequities. And they don't understand race-consciousness itself as an evil.

INQUIRER: Give me a moment here. I want to make sure I understand you. Because, quite frankly, I can't believe you're saying it. If people only knew they were doing something wrong, then they would change. Now, that's what you're saying to me, isn't it?

AUTHOR: Obviously, for some people, it wouldn't make a difference. But what you've said is essentially what I'm saying.

INQUIRER: You don't believe there's hatred and resentment against blacks?

AUTHOR: I know there's hatred and resentment against blacks.

INQUIRER: People who harbor those ill feelings, my friend, ought to know it's wrong to do so. And if they know it's wrong to do so, and yet do it anyway, then they are not misguided, in my opinion. They are plain outright evil and ought to be held accountable for their actions.

AUTHOR: Racial hatred and racial resentment are very strong emotions in the United States. I know that is the case. But most Americans don't hate or resent black people. Most Americans don't hate or resent black people. Most Americans do, however, and you and I are not excluded, most Americans do have race-conscious perceptions, and most Americans do take race into consideration in going about their daily affairs. Now that, in my judgment, is the essence of the racial problem. And yet most Americans don't believe they're doing anything wrong. And even many individuals who reach the point of hatred and resentment don't feel they're doing anything wrong either. You don't accept that. But I think it's so. And it's a sad situation.

INQUIRER: You actually think people don't know it's wrong to hate?

AUTHOR: It's all right to hate the enemy. It's all right to shun and disregard the lowly. That's what I mean when I say it's a sad situation.

INQUIRER: If they don't know what they're doing is wrong, and I'm talking about the racist people of this country, then that's a matter of their own personal misguidance. The fact that a racist is misguided does not excuse his or her conduct. Heck, they're all misguided.

AUTHOR: I'm not saying wrongful conduct should be excused. That's not my position. And you know that's not my position.

INQUIRER: Then why have you bothered to make the point?

AUTHOR: It's no bother.

INQUIRER: If somebody discriminates against me, I'm not about to stop and ask, "Hey, are you misguided?" Misguided or whatever, don't do me wrong. And if you do do me wrong, misguided or whatever, I want satisfaction.

AUTHOR: Uh huh.

INQUIRER: You hear me?

AUTHOR: I hear you.

INQUIRER: Then why do you even make the point that they're misguided?

AUTHOR: Because, as a nation, we are misguided. The hate, the resentment, the race-consciousness, the failure to uplift people from poverty. It's all a matter of misguidance. I don't believe the American people are bad people.

INQUIRER: So what? You don't believe they're bad people. So what?

AUTHOR: Well, your perception of people determines how you approach the overall situation. If you accept the fact that people are misguided, rather than bad or evil, you are more likely to believe there is a solution to the racial problem. You know there's a solution because you know you're dealing with good people. And you know, except for misguidance, that people would come forward and resolve this thing. And because people are misguided, you know the solution to the problem is a matter of destroying misconceptions and pointing out the proper course of action. So, out of the belief that people are good, one can benefit in both confidence and direction: confidence that the problem will be resolved and direction as to how to do it. Now, that's what I believe. And that's why I make the point. And there's something else, too. If you believe whites are evil, you become suspicious, and you develop hostilities such as anger and resentment, not to the detriment of whites, but against your own best interest.

INQUIRER: So blacks should not be suspicious of whites?

AUTHOR: That's certainly part of what I'm saying.

INQUIRER: But, without suspicion, wouldn't blacks be vulnerable and essentially at the mercy of racism?

AUTHOR: That wouldn't be the case.

INQUIRER: That's what you say.

AUTHOR: You deal with each racial situation as you face it. And you protect yourself. But don't live the assumption that all whites are racists. Don't live the assumption that the white population is maliciously motivated against black people.

INQUIRER: Is that what you say blacks are doing?

AUTHOR: Not all blacks are. But some. And that's far too many.

INQUIRER: I agree blacks are watchful of whites, as they should be. I think that's proper. But when you say they "live the assumption", don't you think that's an exaggeration?

AUTHOR: I don't. No, that's not an exaggeration. If you believe white employers are motivated to deny opportunities to black workers, if you believe white workers are racially motivated against black co-workers, if you believe white teachers are motivated to discriminate against black students, if you believe whites who provide service to the public are motivated to be discourteous and unfair to blacks, if you believe merchants are motivated to discriminate against black consumers, if you believe whites who judge and evaluate blacks are motivated to do so unfairly, and if you believe whites in general are motivated to use every opportunity to discredit, unfairly criticize, embarrass, exclude, diminish, deny and even destroy black people, and some blacks do have these beliefs, then you are living the assumption that whites are bad people.

INQUIRER: In view of the things you're saying here, I take it then that you don't think very much of those conspiracy theories.

AUTHOR: Obviously, I don't.

INQUIRER: Well, how do you respond to them? I mean, what thoughts do you have when you hear them being expressed?

AUTHOR: It depends on the theory.

INQUIRER: That the government is trying to destroy blacks with drugs. And that's why so little is being done to drive drugs out of black communities.

AUTHOR: If our government had the desire to destroy its black citizens, it could certainly devise a more effective way of doing so.

INQUIRER: The response to that, of course, is that the government must attack blacks in an indirect fashion. Direct attacks would ignite public opinion against the government's action.

AUTHOR: If public opinion is against attacks on blacks, and the government is for them, then the government would be in opposition to its people. That, of course, could happen. But that's not what we have here.

INQUIRER: I suppose you would have a similar response if someone told you the government was conspiring to keep blacks in poverty, or if someone argued the government was deliberately neglecting crime and disease in black communities.

AUTHOR: I would have a similar response. The problems are certainly there. But they are there as a result of misguidance.

INQUIRER: In your opinion, do businesses conspire to keep blacks in poverty?

AUTHOR: No.

INQUIRER: Is there a conspiracy to discredit black leaders?

AUTHOR: No.

INQUIRER: The mayor of Washington, D.C., a black man, was recently arrested on drug charges. What would you say to those who claim there was a deliberate attempt by the government to discredit this man because he's black?

AUTHOR: What would I say?

INQUIRER: Yes.

AUTHOR: Go on to something else.

INQUIRER: But what is your analysis of that situation?

AUTHOR: The whole idea of blacks as black leaders and black role models is a mistake. Don't build hopes and expectations on the basis of race. When you're in the business of race-consciousness, discredit to one black leader or one role model is discredit to the entire black population. That's just not the way to get things done.

INQUIRER: So, some blacks are suspicious. You say they shouldn't be that way. But they are. And my question to you is this: so what?!

AUTHOR: It's detrimental.

INQUIRER: How? They're not gonna go to heaven or something? Is that what you're talking about?

AUTHOR: If you're going to achieve and succeed in our society, you've got to have some measure of confidence. Because, without confidence, in the extreme case, you accomplish nothing; you're too intimidated by the world to even go out of the house to get a bucket of water. If you're going to succeed in our society, you have to go out and fetch the water, and not only that, but you have the leave the yard and walk down through the woods.

INQUIRER: And I asked you about suspicion. I assume you're in the process of answering my question.

AUTHOR: You have to walk about in the meadows. You have to climb the hills. If, however, you perceive the woods, the creek, the meadows and the hills as unfriendly places, you may not be inclined to go there. And if you do go there, you'd probably be too suspicious to take full advantage of the opportunities presented? You might decline to fish in the creek, for example, feeling you wouldn't catch anything anyway, or that you'd probably catch something that would harm you.

INQUIRER: The point of the whole thing is what?

AUTHOR: If you perceive whites as being evil, your confidence that you can succeed is not going to be that great. After all, how can you succeed with all those people and forces out there against you? And if you don't think you can succeed, you're not going to have the desire or motivation to do so. What's the use? It's not going to work out anyway.

INQUIRER: Let me just clarify something here. You're not talking about self-confidence, are you? I mean, you're not talking about the confidence that one has in his or her own ability?

AUTHOR: I do believe suspicion affects self-confidence. But you're correct, I was speaking of confidence in the American people. And I believe, without that confidence, you're at a great great disadvantage. You have to believe in people. And if you don't, you're not going to be able to set goals, and give your best effort to accomplish those goals. Racial suspicion is lack of confidence. And lack of confidence translates into lost opportunities.

INQUIRER: Your comment that suspicion affects self-confidence?

AUTHOR: Uh huh.

INQUIRER: Your thoughts about that?

AUTHOR: Well, if you feel people are maliciously motivated against you, you may start wondering why, and questioning your own worth. Young people at the critical stage of developing self-confidence would be especially vulnerable to this type of thing. Consider, for example, a young child, a young girl, who comes home from kindergarten having encountered her first significant racial situation. A classmate objects to sitting next to her because of her race. What should the parents say to this young girl? They shouldn't tell her white people hate blacks, don't you agree?

INQUIRER: Why not? And that's not to say I agree or disagree.

AUTHOR: Because that young girl has just been told something is wrong with her. At that point, however, it's just the opinion of one classmate. Don't aggravate the situation. Don't tell her millions of other people feel the same way. You're dealing with her self-confidence. And what you'd want to do in that situation is reassure her.

INQUIRER: How would you do that?

AUTHOR: I'd try to give her something to handle that type of occasion. I'd tell her to disregard, when possible, but to stand strong and not to be intimidated. And I'd tell her that only her classmate and a few other misguided individuals dislike people because of race. I'd tell her that everybody else in the world like people, and do whatever they can to treat people right.

INQUIRER: With that type of advice, you'd be taking a great risk, would you not? If that young girl continues to encounter racial incidents, your advice to her would lose all credibility. Have you any concern about that?

AUTHOR: You ask if there's a risk. Sure, there's a risk. I can only tell you that I believe in people.

INQUIRER: Now, our discussion thus far has been involved primarily with suspicion. But you don't like hate or resentment either.

AUTHOR: Correct.

INQUIRER: And the problem with hate and resentment is what?

AUTHOR: You get preoccupied with hostilities, and you're adversely affected in your personal aspirations. You're too involved with hate and resentment to focus on what you have to do to advance. Also, if you're hateful and resentful, with or without justification, people are uneasy in dealing with you. Consequently, you don't get meaningful consideration for advancement and other opportunities as they become available. And, beyond that, in my opinion, life just can't be that pleasant for individuals who hate and resent other people.

INQUIRER: In considering what you have to say about hate, resentment and suspicion, it appears you believe blacks cause their own problems because they think whites are bad people. And I have to say to you, I think that's a tremendous position for you to take.

AUTHOR: Why did you say that?

INQUIRER: What?

AUTHOR: That I'm saying blacks cause their own problems. You think that's what I said?

INQUIRER: Well, you said life is unpleasant for those who believe people are bad. I mean, with the racist situation what it is, I think you're expecting too much of blacks.

AUTHOR: Now that's fair criticism. And although I don't agree with it, I understand it. But when did I say or even imply blacks cause their own problems?

INQUIRER: Well, that is the implication of what you're saying.

AUTHOR: Absolutely not! I'll respond to any question you have in mind. I don't care. And I know people will disagree with me. But don't unfairly characterize what I'm saying.

INQUIRER: I don't feel it's unfair. You respond to it in whatever fashion you choose.

AUTHOR: Do you really think I am saying blacks cause their own problems?

INQUIRER: I've said what I've said.

AUTHOR: You ought to withdraw it.

INQUIRER: You can respond.

AUTHOR: My comment and my belief is that you adversely affect the quality of your own life when you perceive people as being bad. You're more inclined to hate and resent fellow human beings. You become suspicious, and the world becomes a very hostile place in which to live. Victims of race-conscious practices ought to let the injury end where it ends, and not let our racial situation turn them, the victims, into suspicious, hateful or resentful people. Because when you harbor those hostilities, those hostilities affect you. They are very very demanding, both mentally and emotionally. And they sour your whole outlook on life. It's an awesome burden to carry. And I'll say to anybody who'll listen to me, don't let other people force you to become hateful or resentful. It's a very unpleasant life. And you have a choice. You don't have to live that way.

INQUIRER: You don't mean me, personally?

AUTHOR: What?

INQUIRER: When you say "you."

AUTHOR: Anybody who'll listen to me.

INQUIRER: I mean, you're not saying I'm resentful.

AUTHOR: No.

INQUIRER: Well, that's what I meant.

AUTHOR: Okay.

INQUIRER: Do you say all blacks are hateful and resentful?

AUTHOR: No. I believe I said that. In fact, most people I know are not.

INQUIRER: To what extent, then, do you say these hostilities exist?

AUTHOR: I don't know. But I've seen them. And I tell you, its not a good thing.

INQUIRER: As I said, with the situation as it is, it's difficult for blacks not to harbor hostilities.

AUTHOR: Not only difficult, but as to some situations, impossible.

The best you can do is understand what you must do, and work at it.

INQUIRER: These being your ideas, how have you managed personally, in this regard?

AUTHOR: Okay.

INQUIRER: Any difficulties at all?

AUTHOR: I have those days, as black people do, when something disturbing happens to me, or when I become troubled by a situation or situations. It's a tremendous hurt. And sometimes it shakes you.

INQUIRER: On those occasions, do you ever feel that maybe you're wrong about people?

AUTHOR: I get angry at individuals and situations. There's disappointment. And I become frustrated. I can't say, though, that I've ever given up on people. And I think I've been very fortunate. I continue to encounter warm caring individuals. After a bad experience, a positive encounter can really pick you up. It has done so for me on many occasions. I become rejuvenated.

INQUIRER: What you've just said, I believe, confirms my suspicion: that you have these idealistic beliefs and opinions because you have not been exposed to the realities of racism. It appears, from what I gather, that you've lived what one would call a rather sheltered life.

AUTHOR: I don't agree with that.

Inquirer: I didn't expect you would.

AUTHOR: Look, I'm not inclined to compare my hardships or experiences to those of others, but I'll tell you this, and you make whatever judgment you please, I have been out in the rain. I continue to be out there. My life has not been sheltered.

INQUIRER: That's your opinion.

AUTHOR: It is indeed my opinion. It happens also to be a fact.

INQUIRER: Well, then, let me ask you some specific questions about that.

AUTHOR: All right.

INQUIRER: You turned eighteen in December of 1964, so you were born in '46?

AUTHOR: That's correct.

INQUIRER: Where were you born?

AUTHOR: In Georgia. Carroll County, Georgia. And that's about sixty miles southwest of Atlanta.

INQUIRER: Do you have brothers and sisters?

AUTHOR: Eleven.

INQUIRER: Any of them lawyers?

AUTHOR: No, they're not lawyers.

INQUIRER: Tell me about your parents.

AUTHOR: My mother continues to do domestic work and some babysitting around and about. And my father is now retired.

INQUIRER: From what occupation?

AUTHOR: Mechanical work on school buses. He was employed by the County. Now, that's a job he took, I believe, in the late sixties. Before that, he was a sharecropper.

INQUIRER: A sharecropper.

AUTHOR: Yes.

INQUIRER: During what period of time?

AUTHOR: All his life, until the late sixties as I said.

INQUIRER: That would mean, I guess, that you grew up as a sharecropper?

AUTHOR: That's correct.

INQUIRER: I don't have to tell you that that surprises me. Well, tell me about you personally in that situation.

AUTHOR: What situation?

INQUIRER: Sharecropping.

AUTHOR: What do you want to know?

INQUIRER: You can begin by describing in general what sharecropping involved.

AUTHOR: Well, a farmer would have some land available for the growing of certain crops. There would be mules, cows, wagons, plows and other farm equipment, and there would usually be two houses: one in which the farmer and his family would reside, and the other would be for the sharecroppers. The sharecroppers would move in and grow and harvest crops on the land. Any profits from the crops, after expenses, would be equally divided. Now, that was the basic arrangement. And the primary crops for us were corn and cotton.

INQUIRER: You mentioned profits. Was there truly a profit in it for the sharecropper? My understanding is that there was not.

AUTHOR: Some money was usually available in the fall, after the cotton was sold. We got new shoes and clothes and there were things for Christmas. But I'd have to agree with you, soon after Christmas, you'd start looking towards the next harvest.

INQUIRER: So, at that point, how did you live?

AUTHOR: Corn bread, milk, butter, eggs, chickens, hogs, I mean, these things were available on the farm. And, of course, we grew potatoes and other vegetables. Many vegetables, as I recall, were canned during the summer and stored away for the winter.

INQUIRER: There still must've been a need for money. You had cars, I assume. And there must've been medical expenses, electric bills, and things like that.

AUTHOR: My mother did some domestic work, as I said. And there were periods of time when there was nothing to do on the farm but wait for the crops to mature, or wait for spring to begin plowing the fields. And my father would look, during these periods of time, for day-to-day work elsewhere.

INQUIRER: Was that sufficient?

AUTHOR: Well, if you couldn't manage with that, you'd borrow money from the farmer with whom you were sharecropping.

INQUIRER: And you'd pay that money back when the crops were sold?

AUTHOR: Yes.

INQUIRER: And some sharecroppers, as I understand it, after paying off their debts, had little or no money left at all, or perhaps were not even able to pay off their debts. Do you have any personal knowledge of that?

AUTHOR: I believe my family was always able to at least get something.

INQUIRER: As you think back on your life as a sharecropper, and I know you've done that, can you pin point the time when you first realized something was wrong?

AUTHOR: You mean, something wrong racially?

INQUIRER: Yes.

AUTHOR: That was not an immediate thing. The whites you came into contact with were usually courteous and pleasant, within the accepted customs and practices. And it didn't occur to me, in the beginning, that those customs and practices were wrong. You were born into a situation and things were the way they were.

INQUIRER: I understand what you're saying.

AUTHOR: Now, in the case of poverty, that's an entirely different story. I knew from the very beginning that there was something terribly wrong with people having to live the way we lived.

INQUIRER: But you didn't attribute that to racism?

AUTHOR: In the beginning, I don't believe so.

INQUIRER: What specifically were the conditions of poverty for you and your family? There wasn't a problem with food, I take it. You indicated before that you lived essentially off the land.

AUTHOR: I wouldn't go so far, though, as to glorify that aspect of our lives. There were days of milk and bread and sugar biscuits.

INQUIRER: I would expect there were. I'm not insensitive, believe me, I'm just trying to understand the conditions.

AUTHOR: Ten to twelve hours work each day during the summer months, the hot weather, mules and plows in the fields, chopping and picking cotton, pulling corn, hauling hay, and other jobs around and about. The work was enormous.

INQUIRER: What else?
AUTHOR: The housing situation was bad.
INQUIRER: How?
AUTHOR: Leaky roofs, holes and cracks in the walls and floors, and things like that. Not very pleasing to look at. And with the wind coming through the cracks and all, it was difficult to keep warm during the winter.
INQUIRER: Okay.
AUTHOR: And we had those rats just running around in the house. Also, we had those chinches.
INQUIRER: Chinches?
AUTHOR: Yes.
INQUIRER: Did you say chinches?
AUTHOR: Yes.
INQUIRER: I don't know what chinches are?
AUTHOR: You mean you don't know what chinches are?
INQUIRER: Perhaps by another name.
AUTHOR: No, I don't think so. If you'd met 'em, that's what you'd call 'em.
INQUIRER: What are they?
AUTHOR: Bed bugs. They'd hide in cracks and corners during the day, and at night when you lie down to sleep, they'd come out and feast. You understand, don't you?
INQUIRER: Well, couldn't you kill these things or something?
AUTHOR: You betcha you killed them. Sucking your blood like that.
INQUIRER: Well, let me get back to my question here. You say in the beginning you did not realize something was wrong.
AUTHOR: Racially.
INQUIRER: That's what I mean.
AUTHOR: As I think back, that's the way I remember it.
INQUIRER: But there did come a time when you did have that realization.
AUTHOR: Obviously.
INQUIRER: My question is when. When did you first realize something was wrong racially?
AUTHOR: I don't think you can say a particular day or hour, or anything like that. It's a realization that you come to gradually. You mature and you learn. And you're exposed to certain realities. But there is a day that I remember. And after that day, I can tell you for sure, there was no question in my mind that something very unpleasant was going on.
INQUIRER: What happened?
AUTHOR: We were picking cotton. And my mother drove up on the road nearby, got out of the car and walked across the field to my father.

Young white boys in another car had confronted her and called her derogatory names. As she told my father what happened, I could see that she was deeply hurt. And I didn't like that at all.

INQUIRER: How old were you at that time?

AUTHOR: I don't remember that.

INQUIRER: Nine? Ten? Eleven?

AUTHOR: I guess.

INQUIRER: Tell me about your relationship with whites after that experience.

AUTHOR: Well, you didn't usually have a whole lot of contact with them.

INQUIRER: But they lived all around you, did they not?

AUTHOR: That is the case. And you saw them. But generally, you didn't become involved in any way. As I grew older, however, I did start to have more involvement.

INQUIRER: How did that come about?

AUTHOR: Well, just growing up and going out into the world, taking care of various personal affairs, working odd jobs, and things like that, you were involved necessarily with whites.

INQUIRER: And, as you moved out into the world at that time, what was your perception of white people?

AUTHOR: I was apprehensive.

INQUIRER: Did you have bad experiences?

AUTHOR: You'd have to know I did. But they weren't all bad.

INQUIRER: Although you don't now, did you at that time consider whites bad or evil people?

AUTHOR: I can't say that I did. I was certainly hurt and angered, and many times also frightened. And I'd become frustrated, like I get today. I can't say though that I considered them bad or evil people. Even with things the way they were, I did have positive relationships with some whites.

INQUIRER: After you realized something was wrong racially, did you then have any thoughts at all about taking action to correct the situation?

AUTHOR: Obviously, I wanted things to be right. But I didn't envision that it was for me to make them right. I never made a pledge to myself that I would resolve the racial problem. I certainly had dreams at that time, but my focus was not on race relations.

INQUIRER: What dreams did you have?

AUTHOR: That I would do something, and I didn't know what, but that I would do something to uplift my mother, my father and my brothers and sisters out of poverty. And that I would do something very positive with my own life.

INQUIRER: Like what?

AUTHOR: That I would accomplish something.

INQUIRER: Like what?

AUTHOR: In my thoughts, it was many things. I would invent something. I would become a Doctor, a scientist, a pilot. Many things came to mind.

INQUIRER: Did you feel as a youngster that you could actually accomplish what you wanted?

AUTHOR: Yes.

INQUIRER: How?

AUTHOR: I didn't know how, except we were told by our parents and our teachers that it was important to get a good education.

Inquirer: To get a good education?

AUTHOR: Yes.

INQUIRER: But did that really mean anything to you, in your situation?

AUTHOR: It did.

INQUIRER: What?

AUTHOR: To go as far as we could to graduate from high school.

INQUIRER: And to graduate from high school is something you wanted to do?

AUTHOR: Yes.

INQUIRER: Now, the Supreme Court declared segregated schools unconstitutional in 1954. You were school age at that time, and being in Georgia, you were probably attending a racially segregated school.

AUTHOR: That's correct.

INQUIRER: Tell me about your school.system as you grew up.

AUTHOR: Well, there were five or six, I don't recall the exact number, elementary schools in the County for black students. There was one high school. And students were bussed to the various schools. That's essentially the way it was.

INQUIRER: When were the schools in your county integrated?

AUTHOR: A year or two, I believe, after I enlisted into the Air Force.

INQUIRER: You graduated from a segregated high school?

AUTHOR: Yes.

INQUIRER: Now, aside from the inequality as a result of the segregation, was there any further difficulty for you because you were a sharecropper?

AUTHOR: Many blacks were sharecroppers. I don't want you to think we were the only sharecroppers.

INQUIRER: I understand that. I just want to know if there was any further difficulty. That may not have been the case.

AUTHOR: Well, parents kept their kids out of school to pick cotton. They really didn't have a choice in that.

INQUIRER: Were you kept out of school?

AUTHOR: Yes.
INQUIRER: How much time did you lose?
AUTHOR: Two or three months, I suppose.
INQUIRER: Out of each school year?
AUTHOR: Yes.
INQUIRER: That's a considerable amount of time.
AUTHOR: That's the way it was.
INQUIRER: How did you pursue your dreams and aspirations after you graduated from high school?
AUTHOR: I didn't?
INQUIRER: Not at all?
AUTHOR: Immediately after high school, I didn't.
INQUIRER: What did you do?
AUTHOR: I went to work at this Company.
INQUIRER: Anything else?
AUTHOR: You mean my personal life?
INQUIRER: Your personal life is precisely what we're talking about.
AUTHOR: Well, I had become involved at that time actually in what one may consider a very unhealthy way of life.
INQUIRER: What did you get involved in?
AUTHOR: Knives, guns, whiskey, beer, or whatever, going to various dances, clubs and other places for entertainment, and generally living sort of a wild life.
INQUIRER: What did you do with the knives and guns?
AUTHOR: You'd fight.
INQUIRER: Who would you fight?
AUTHOR: Whoever made you mad.
INQUIRER: How did you get involved in this unhealthy way of life, as you call it?
AUTHOR: I don't know. It was just there and I stepped right in. Or maybe it came to me. I just don't know. "Way of life" is a good way to describe it. That's exactly what it was, a way of life. And in fact, it still is for a lot of people. You moved around to the various places and established your own reputation. And that reputation was important to you. You had to show people you couldn't be pushed around. You were a somebody in the world. And people had to know that.
INQUIRER: And in these fights you mentioned, I assume people got hurt?
AUTHOR: Yes.
INQUIRER: And I assume also that one could have gotten himself killed?
AUTHOR: That happened.
INQUIRER: What were your thoughts at that time about your dreams, the things you wanted to do with your life?

AUTHOR: That I still wanted to do them.

INQUIRER: But you weren't trying.

AUTHOR: That's true.

INQUIRER: Why not?

AUTHOR: Well, I had graduated from high school. And the people I knew didn't go beyond that.

INQUIRER: But you were different. Didn't you think that?

AUTHOR: I had not been introduced to possibilities in college. And I didn't seek out those possibilities.

INQUIRER: But why? That's the question, isn't it? Why didn't you seek out possibilities in college?

AUTHOR: I was frightened and intimidated, I suppose, by the very thought of reaching out into the world. And I just got caught up in the life I could see right there in front of me.

INQUIRER: I take it then that you gave up on yourself, at least at that particular time?

AUTHOR: I still felt I would reach out.

INQUIRER: And, obviously, you did eventually reach out. When and how did that occur?

AUTHOR: As I mentioned before, I enlisted into the Air Force in December of 1964.

INQUIRER: I can tell by what you say that you consider that a turning point in your life.

AUTHOR: I do.

INQUIRER: Why?

AUTHOR: Because, although I continued to drink and live that wild type of life, the Air Force introduced me to new people, new ideas, new places, new possibilities, and just opened up the world to me. And towards the end of my enlistment, I found in my association with certain people encouragement and inspiration to go on to college and continue my education.

INQUIRER: Now I think you'd probably agree that people who grow up in poverty, as you did, don't usually become lawyers? And I'm just wondering, in your own mind, what you think made the difference for you.

AUTHOR: I was fortunate.

INQUIRER: Don't you think your dreams, as you call them, had something to do with it?

AUTHOR: Obviously, I do.

INQUIRER: What do you think your life would have been like had you not pursued your dreams?

AUTHOR: One can only guess.

INQUIRER: While you were living that unhealthy way of life, before you joined the Air Force, did you ever have any thoughts that you'd kill somebody, or perhaps end up dead yourself?

AUTHOR: I had those thoughts.

INQUIRER: What role, if any, did those thoughts play in your ultimate decision to move on?

AUTHOR: A sense of urgency, I suppose. Just before I enlisted, I did feel a sense of urgency.

INQUIRER: Can you be any more specific than that?

AUTHOR: Let me tell you about an incident. I was on my way home on a back road one Sunday night, and a car came up behind me blinking its headlights. I thought it was a state trooper and I pulled over and got out of my car. The driver of that other car also got out and his headlights were sort of blinding me. I heard the clicking sound of a gun. I knew it was a shot gun. I thought I was going to die. Now, I had certainly been in confrontations before that involving knives and guns, but this one was different. I thought I was going to die. And I knew right then and there that I didn't want to die like that.

INQUIRER: What happened?

AUTHOR: He called my name.

INQUIRER: Did you know him?

AUTHOR: Yes.

INQUIRER: Why was he after you?

AUTHOR: Two nights before that, a friend of mine had shot at him. We didn't know whether or not he was hit. He'd gotten away in a car.

INQUIRER: So, he was after your friend. He wasn't looking for you.

AUTHOR: You'll never convince me of that. He wanted both of us.

INQUIRER: Why?

AUTHOR: Well, it all began when the guy came to a place with a girl that I had an interest in. My friend was offended by it all and just took the guy on.

INQUIRER: You and the guy with the shot gun. What happened that night?

AUTHOR: He let me go.

APPENDIX

PLESSY V FERGUSON
U.S. Supreme Court 1896

Mr. Justice Harlan dissenting.

By the Louisiana statute the validity of which is here involved, all railway companies (other than street-railroad companies) carrying passengers in that state are required to have separate but equal accommodations for white and colored persons, "by providing two or more passenger coaches for each passenger train, or by dividing the passenger coaches by a partition so as to secure separate accommodations." Under this statute, no colored person is permitted to occupy a seat in a coach assigned to white persons; nor any white person to occupy a seat in a coach assigned to colored persons. The managers of the railroad are not allowed to exercise any discretion in the premises, but are required to assign each passenger to some coach or compartment set apart for the exclusive use of his race. If a passenger insists upon going into a coach or compartment not set apart for persons of his race, he is subject to be fined, or to be imprisoned in the parish jail. Penalties are prescribed for the refusal or neglect of the officers, directors, conductors, and employes of railroad companies to comply with the provisions of the act.

Only "nurses attending children of the other race" are excepted from the operation fo the statute. No exception is made of colored attendants travelling with adults. A white man is not permitted to have his colored servant with him in the same coach, even if his condition of health requires the constant personal assistance of such servant. If a colored maid insists upon riding in the same coach with a white woman whom she has been employed to serve, and who may need her personal attention while travelling, she is subject to be fined or imprisoned for such an exhibition of zeal in the discharge of duty.

While there may be in Louisiana persons of different races who are not citizens of the United States, the words in the act "white and colored races" necessarily include all citizens of the United States of both races residing in that state. So that we have before us a state enactment that compels, under penalties, the separation of the two races in railroad passenger coaches, and makes it a crime for a citizen of either race to enter a coach that has been assigned to citizens of the other race.

Thus, the state regulates the use of a public highway by citizens of the United States solely upon the basis of race.

However apparent the injustice of such legislation may be, we have only to consider whether it is consistent with the constitution of the United States.

That a railroad is a public highway, and that the corporation which owns or operates it is in the exercise of public functions, is not, at this day, to be disputed. Mr. Justice Nelson, speaking for this court in *New Jersey Steam Nav. Co. v. Merchants' Bank*, 6 How. 344, 382, said that a common carrier was in the exercise "of a sort of public office, and has public duties to perform, from which he should not be permitted to exonerate himself without the assent of the parties concerned." Mr. Justice Strong, delivering the judgment of this court in *Olcott v. Supervisors*, 16 Wall. 678, 694, said: "That railroads, though constructed by private corporations, and owned by them, are public highways, has been the doctrine of nearly all the courts ever since such conveniences for passage and transportation have had any existence. Very early the question arose whether a state's right of eminent domain could be exercised by a private corporation created for the purpose of constructing a railroad. Clearly, it could not, unless taking land for such a purpose by such an agency is taking land for public use. The right of eminent domain nowhere justifies taking property for a private use. Yet it is a doctrine universally accepted that a state legislature may authorize a private corporation to take land for the construction of such a road, making compensation to the owner. What else does this doctrine mean if not that building a railroad, though it be built by a private corporation, is an act done for a public use?" So, in *Township of Pine Grove v. Talcott*, 19 Wall. 666, 676: "Though the corporation [a railroad company] was private, its work was public, as much so as if it were to be constructed by the state." So, in *Inhabitants of Worcester v. Western R. Corp.*, 4 Metc. (Mass.) 564: "The establishment of that great thoroughfare is regarded as a public work, established by public authority, intended for the public use and benefit, the use of which is secured to the whole community, and constitutes, therefore, like a canal, turnpike, or highway, a public easement." "It is true that the real and personal property, necessary to the establishment and management of the railroad, is vested in the corporation; but it is in trust for the public."

In respect of civil rights, common to all citizens, the constitution of the United States does not, I think, permit any public authority to know the race of those entitled to be protected in the enjoyment of such rights. Every true man has pride of race, and under appropriate circumstances, when the rights of others, his equals before the law, are not to be affected, it is his privilege to express such pride and to take such action based upon it as to him seems proper. But I deny that any legislative body or judicial tribunal may have regard to the race of citizens when the civil rights of those citizens are involved. Indeed, such legislation as that here in question is inconsistent not only with that equality of rights which pertains to citizenship, national and state, but with the personal liberty enjoyed by every one within the United States.

The Thirteenth Amendment does not permit the withholding or the deprivation of any right necessarily inhering in freedom. It not only struck down the institution of slavery as previously existing in the United States, but it prevents the imposition of any burdens or disabilities that constitute badges of slavery or servitude. It decreed universal civil freedom in this country. This court has so adjudged. But, that amendment having been found inadequate to the protection fo the rights of those who had been in slavery, it was followed by the Fourteenth Amendment, which added greatly to the dignity and glory of American citizenship, and to the security of personal liberty, by declaring that "all persons born or naturalized in the United States, and subject to the jurisdiction thereof, are citizens of the United States and of the state wherein they reside," and that "no state shall make or enforce any law which shall abridge the privileges or immunities of citizens of the United States; nor shall any state deprive any person of life, liberty or property without due process of law, nor deny to any person within its jurisdiction the equal protection of the laws." These two amendments, if enforced according to their true intent and meaning, will protect all the civil rights that pertain to freedom and citizenship. Finally, and to the end that no citizen should be denied, on account of his race, the privilege of participating in the political control of his country, it was declared by the Fifteenth Amendment that "the right of citizens of the United States to vote shall not be denied or abridged by the United States or by any state on account of race, color or previous condition of servitude."

These notable additions to the fundamental law were welcomed by the friends of liberty throughout the world. They removed the race line from our governmental systems. They had, as this court has said, a common purpose, namely, to secure "to a race recently emancipated, a race that through many generations have been held in slavery, all the civil rights that the superior race enjoy." They declared, in legal effect, this court has further said, "that the law in the states shall be the same for the black as for the white; that all persons, whether colored or white, shall stand equal before the laws of the states; and in regard to the colored race, for whose protection the amendment was primarily designed, that no discrimination shall be made against them by law because of their color." We also said: "The words of the amendment, it is true, are prohibitory, but they contain a necessary implication of a positive immunity or right, most valuable to the colored race,—the right to exemption from unfriendly legislation against them distinctively as colored; exemption from legal discriminations, implying inferiority in civil society, lessening the security of their enjoyment of the rights which others enjoy; and discriminations which are steps towards reducing them to the condition of a subject race." It was, consequently, adjudged that a state law that excluded citizens of the colored race from juries, because of their race, however well qualified in other respects to discharge the duties of jurymen, was repugnant to the Fourteenth Amendment. *Strauder v. West Virginia*, 100 U. S. 303, 306, 307; *Virginia v. Rives*,Id. 313; *Ex parte Virginia*, Id 339; *Neal v. Delaware*, 103 U.S. 370, 386; *Bush v. Kentucky.*, 107 U. S. 110, 116, 1 Sup. Ct. 625. At the present term, referring to the previous adjudications, this court declared that "underlying all of those decisions is the principle that the constitution of the United States, in its present form, forbids, so far as civil and political rights are concerned, discrimination by the general government or the states against any citizen because of his race. All citizens are equal before the law." *Gibson v. Mississippi* 162 U. S. 565, 16 sup. Ct. 904.

The decision referred to show the scope of the recent amendments of the constitution. They also show that it is not within the power of a state to prohibit colored citizens, because of their race, from participating as jurors in the administration of justice.

It was said in argument that the statute of Louisiana does not discriminate against either race, but prescribes a rule applicable alike to white and colored citizens. But his argument does not meet the difficulty. Everyone knows that the statute in question had its origin in the purpose, not so much to exclude white persons from railroad cars occupied by blacks, as to exclude colored people from coaches occupied by or assigned to white persons. Railroad corporations of Louisiana did not make discrimination among whites in the matter of accommodation for travelers. The thing to accomplish was, under the guise of giving equal accommodation for whites and blacks, to compel the latter to keep to themselves while traveling in railroad passenger coaches. No one would be so wanting in candor as to assert the contrary. The fundamental objection, therefore, to the statute, is that it interferes with the personal freedom of citizens. "Personal liberty," it has been well said, "consists in the power of locomotion, of changing situation, or removing one's person to whatsoever places one's own inclination may direct, without imprisonment or restraint, unless by due course of law." 1 Bl. Comm. 134. If a white man and a black man choose to occupy the same public conveyance on a public highway, it is their right to do so; and no government, proceeding alone on grounds of race, can prevent it without infringing the personal liberty of each.

It is one thing for railroad carriers to furnish, or to be required by law to furnish, equal accommodations for all whom they are under a legal duty to carry. It is quite another thing for government to forbid citizens of the white and black races from traveling in the same public conveyance, and to punish officers of railroad companies for permitting persons of the two races to occupy the same passenger coach. If a state can prescribe, as a rule of civil conduct, that whites and blacks shall not travel as passengers in the same railroad coach, why may it not so regulate the use of the streets of its cities and towns as to compel white citizens to keep on one side of a street, and black citizens to keep on the other? Why may it not, upon like grounds, punish white and blacks who ride together in street cars or in open vehicles on a public road or street? Why may it not require sheriffs to assign whites to one side of a court room, and blacks to the other? And why may it not also prohibit the commingling of the two races in the galleries of legislative halls or in public assemblages convened for the consideration of the political questions of the day? Further, if this statute of Louisiana is consistent with the personal liberty of citizens, why may not the state require the separation in railroad coaches of native and naturalized citizens of the United States, or of Protestants and Roman Catholics?

The answer given at the argument to these questions was that regulations of the kind they suggest would be unreasonable, and could not, therefore, stand before the law. Is it meant that the determination of questions of legislative power depends upon the inquiry whether the statute whose validity is questioned is, in the judgment of the courts, a reasonable one, taking all the circumstances into consideration? A statute may be unreasonable merely because a sound public policy forbade its enactment. But I do not understand that the courts have anything to do with the policy or expediency of legislation. A statute may be valid, and yet, upon grounds of public policy, may well be characterized as unreasonable. Mr. Sedgwick correctly states the rule when he says that the legislative intention being clearly ascertained, "the courts have no other duty to perform than to execute the legislative will, without regard to their views as to the wisdom or justice of the particular enactment." Stat. & Const. Constr. 324. There is a dangerous tendency in these latter days to enlarge the functions of the courts, by means of judicial interference with the will of the people as expressed by the legislature. Our institutions have the distinguishing characteristic that the three departments of government are coordinate and separate. Each must keep within the limits defined by the Constitution. And the courts best discharge their duty by executing the will of the law-making power, constitutionally expressed, leaving the results of legislation to be dealt with by the people through their representatives. Statutes must always have a reasonable construction. Sometimes they are to be construed strictly; sometimes, liberally, in order to carry out the legislative will. But however construed, the intent of the legislature is to be respected, if the particular statute in question is valid, although the courts, looking at the public interests, may conceive the statute to be both unreasonable and impolitic. If the power exists to enact a statute, that ends the matter so far as the courts are concerned. The adjudged cases in which statutes have been held to be void, because unreasonable, are those in which the means employed by legislature were not at all germane to the end to which the legislature was competent.

The white race deems itself to be the dominant race in this country. And so it is, in prestige, in achievements, in education, in wealth and in power. So, I doubt not, it will continue to be for all time, if it remains true to its great heritage and holds fast to the principles of constitutional liberty. But in view of the Constitution, in the eye of the law, there is in this country no superior, dominant, ruling class of citizens. There is no caste here. Our Constitution is color-blind, and neither knows nor tolerates classes among citizens. In respect of civil rights, all citizens are equal before the law. The humblest is the peer of the most powerful. The law regards man as man, and takes no account of his surroundings or of his color when his civil rights as guaranteed by the supreme law of the land are involved. It is, therefore, to be regretted that this high tribunal, the final expositor of the fundamental law of the land, has reached the conclusion that it is competent for a State to regulate the enjoyment by citizens of their civil rights solely upon the basis of race.

In my opinion, the judgment this day rendered will, in time, prove to be quite as pernicious as the decision made by this tribunal in the Dred Scott case. It was adjudged in that case that the descendants of Africans who were imported into this country and sold as slaves were not included nor intended to be included under the word "citizens" in the Constitution, and could not claim any of the rights and privileges which that instrument provided for and secured to citizens of the United States; that at the time of the adoption of the Constitution they were "considered as a subordinate and inferior class of beings, who had be subjugated by the dominant race, and, whether emancipated or not, yet remained subject to their authority, and had no rights or privileges but such as those who held the power and the government might choose to grant them." 19 How. 393, 404. The recent amendments to the Constitution, it was supposed, had eradicated these principles from our institutions. But it seems that we have yet, in some of the States, a dominant race—a superior class of citizens, which assumes to regulate the enjoyment of civil rights, common to all citizens, upon the basis of race. The present decision, it may well be apprehended, will not only stimulate aggression, more or less brutal and irritating, upon the admitted rights of colored citizens, but will encourage the belief that it is possible, by means of state enactments, to defeat the beneficent purposes which the people of the United States had in view when they adopted the recent amendments of the Constitution, by one of which the blacks of this country were made citizens of the United States and of the States in which they respectively reside, and whose privileges and immunities, as citizens, the States are forbidden to abridge. Sixty millions of whites are in no danger from the presence here of eight millions of blacks. The destinies of the two races, in this country, are indissolubly linked together, and the interests of both require that the common government of all shall not permit the seeds of race hate to be planted under the sanction of law. What can more certainly arouse race hate, what more certainly create and perpetuate a feeling of distrust between these races, than state enactments, which, in fact, proceed on the ground that colored citizens are so inferior and degraded that they cannot be allowed to sit in public coaches occupied by white citizens? That, as all will admit, is the real meaning of such legislation as was enacted in Louisiana.

The sure guarantee of the peace and security of each race is clear, distinct, unconditional recognition by our governments, National and State, of every right that inheres in civil freedom, and of the equality before the law of all citizens of the United States without regard to race. State enactments, regulating the enjoyment of civil rights, upon the basis of race, and cunningly devised to defeat legitimate results of the war, under the pretence of recognizing equality of rights, can have no other result than to render permanent peace impossible, and to keep alive a conflict of races, the continuance of which must do harm to all concerned. This question is not met by the suggestion that social equality cannot exist between the white and black races in this country. That argument, if it can be properly regarded as one, is scarcely worthy of consideration; for social equality no more exists between two races when travelling in a passenger coach or a public highway than when members of the same races sit by each other in a street car or in the jury box, or stand or sit with each other in a political assembly, or when they use in common the streets of a city or town, or when they are in the same room for the purpose of having their names placed on the registry of voters, or when they approach the ballot-box in order to exercise the high privilege of voting.

There is a race so different from our own that we do not permit those belonging to it to become citizens of the United States. Persons belonging to it are, with few exceptions, absolutely excluded from our country. I allude to the Chinese race. But by the statute in question, a Chinaman can ride in the same passenger coach with white citizens of the United States, while citizens of the black race in Louisiana, many of whom, perhaps, risked their lives for the preservation of the Union, who are entitled, by law, to participate in the political control of the State and nation, who are not excluded, by law or by reason of their race, from public stations of any kind, and who have all the legal rights that belong to white citizens, are yet declared to be criminals, liable to imprisonment, if they ride in a public coach occupied by citizens of the white race. It is scarcely just to say that a colored citizen should not object to occupying a public coach assigned to his own race. He does not object, nor, perhaps, would he object to separate coaches for his race, if his rights under the law were recognized. But he objects, and ought never to cease objecting to the proposition, that citizens of the white and black races can be adjudged criminals because they sit, or claim the right to sit, in the same public coach on a public highway.

The arbitrary separation of citizens, on the basis of race, while they are on a public highway, is a badge of servitude wholly inconsistent with the civil freedom and the equality before the law established by the Constitution. It cannot be justified upon any legal grounds.

If evils will result from the commingling of the two races upon public highways established for the benefit of all, they will be infinitely less than those that will surely come from state legislation regulating the enjoyment of civil rights on the basis of race. We boast of the freedom enjoyed by our people above all other peoples. But it is difficult to reconcile that boast with a state of law which, practically, puts the brand of servitude and degradation upon a large class of our fellow-citizens, our equals before the law. The thin disguise of "equal" accommodations for passengers in railroad coaches will not mislead anyone, nor atone for the wrong this day done.

The result of the whole matter is, that while this court has frequently adjudged, and at the present term has recognized the doctrine, that a State cannot, consistently with the Constitution of the United States, prevent white and black citizens, having the required qualifications for jury service, from sitting in the same jury box, it is now solemnly held that a State may prohibit white and black citizens from sitting in the same passenger coach on a public highway, or may require that they be separated by a "partition", when in the same passenger coach. May it not now be reasonably expected that astute men of the dominant race, who affect to be disturbed at the possibility that the integrity of the white race may be corrupted, or that its supremacy will be imperilled, by contact on public highways with black people, will endeavor to procure statutes requiring white and black jurors to be separated in the jury box by a "partition", and that, upon retiring from the court room to consult as to their verdict, such partition, if it be a moveable one, shall be taken to their consultation room, and set up in such way as to prevent black jurors from coming too close to their brother jurors of the white race. If the "partition" used in the court room happens to be stationary, provision could be made for screens with openings through which jurors of the two races could confer as to their verdict without coming into personal contact with each other. I cannot see but that, according to the principles this day announced, such state legislation, although conceived in hostility to, and enacted for the purpose of humiliating citizens of the United States of a particular race, would be held to be consistent with the Constitution.

I do not deem it necessary to review the decisions of state courts to which reference was made in argument. Some, and the most important, of them are wholly inapplicable, because rendered prior to the adoption of the last amendments of the Constitution, when colored people had very few rights which the dominant race felt obliged to respect. Others were made at a time when public opinion, in many localities, was dominated by the institution of slavery; when it would not have been safe to do justice to the black man; and when, so far as the rights of blacks were concerned, race prejudice was, practically, the supreme law of the land. Those decisions cannot be guides in the era introduced by the recent amendments of the supreme law, which established universal civil freedom, gave citizenship to all born or naturalized in the United States and residing here, obliterated the race line from our systems of governments, National and State, and placed our free institutions upon the broad and sure foundation of the equality of all men before the law.

I am of opinion that the statute of Louisiana is inconsistent with the personal liberty of citizens, white and black, in that State, and hostile to both the spirit and letter of the Constitution of the United States. If laws of like character should be enacted in the several States of the Union, the effect would be in the highest degree mischievous. Slavery, as an institution tolerated by law would, it is true, have disappeared from our country, but there would remain a power in the States, by sinister legislation, to interfere with the full enjoyment of the blessings of freedom; to regulate civil rights, common to all citizens, upon the basis of race; and to place in a condition of legal inferiority a large body of American citizens, now constituting a part of the political community called the People of the United States, for whom, and by whom through representatives, our government is administered. Such a system is inconsistent with the guarantee given by the Constitution to each State of a republican form of government, and may be stricken down by Congressional action, or by the courts in the discharge of their solemn duty to maintain the supreme law of the land, anything in the constitution or laws of any State to the contrary notwithstanding.

For the reasons stated, I am constrained to withhold by assent from the opinion and judgment of the majority.

BROWN V BOARD OF EDUCATION
U.S. Supreme Court 1954

Mr. Chief Justice Warren delivered the opinion of the Court.

These cases come to us from the States of Kansas, South Carolina, Virginia, and Delaware. They are premised on different facts and different local conditions, but a common legal question justifies their consolidated opinion.

In each of the cases, minors of the Negro race, through their legal representatives, seek the aid of the courts in obtaining admission to the public schools of their community on a nonsegregated basis. In each instance, they had been denied admission to schools attended by white children under laws requiring or permitting segregation according to race. This segregation was alleged to deprive the plaintiffs of the equal protection of the laws under the Fourteenth Amendment. In each of the cases other than the Delaware case, a three-judge federal district court denied the relief to the plaintiffs on the so-called "separate but equal" doctrine announced by this Court in *Plessy v. Ferguson*, 163 U.S 537. Under that doctrine, equality of treatment is accorded when the races are provided substantially equal facilities, even though these facilities be separate. In the Delaware case, the Supreme Court of Delaware adhered to that doctrine, but ordered that the plaintiffs be admitted to the white schools because of their superiority to the Negro schools.

The plaintiffs contend that segregated public schools are not "equal" and cannot be made "equal", and that hence they are deprived of the equal protection of the laws. Because of the obvious importance of the question presented, the Court took jurisdiction. Argument was heard in the 1952 Term, and reargument was heard this Term on certain questions propounded by the Court.

Regargument was largely devoted to the circumstances surrounding the adoption of the Fourteenth Amendment in 1868. It covered exhaustively consideration of the Amendment in Congress, ratification by the states, then existing practices in racial segregation, and the views of proponents and opponents of the Amendment. This discussion and our own investigation convince us that, although these sources cast some light, it is not enough to resolve the problem with which we are faced. At best, they are inconclusive. The most avid proponents of the post-War Amendments undoubtedly intended them to remove all legal distinctions among "all persons born or naturalized in the United States." Their opponents, just as certainly, were antagonistic to both the letter and the spirit of the Amendments and wished them to have the most limited effect. What others in Congress and the state legislatures had in mind cannot be determined with any degree of certainty.

An additional reason for the inconclusive nature of the Amendment's history, with respect to segregated schools, is the status of public education at that time. In the South, the movement toward free common schools, supported by general taxation, had not yet taken hold. Education of white children was largely in the hands of private groups. Education of Negroes was almost nonexistent, and practically all of the race were illiterate. In fact, any education of Negroes was forbidden by law in some states. Today, in contrast, many Negroes have achieved outstanding success in the arts and sciences as well as in the business and profession world. It is true that public school education at the time of the Amendment had advanced further in the North, but the effect of the Amendment on Northern States was generally ignored in the congressional debates. Even in the North, the conditions of public education did not approximate those existing today. The curriculum was usually rudimentary; ungraded schools were common in rural areas; the school term was but three months a year in many states; and compulsory school attendance was virtually unknown. As a consequence, it is not surprising that there should be so little in the history of the Fourteenth Amendment relating to its intended effect on public education.

In the first cases in this Court construing the Fourteenth Amendment, decided shortly after its adoption, the Court interpreted it as proscribing all state-imposed discrimination against the Negro race. The doctrine of "separate but equal" did not make its appearance in this court until 1896 in the case of *Plessy v. Ferguson, supra* involving not education but transportation. American courts have since labored with the doctrine for over half a century. In this Court, there have been six cases involving the "separate but equal" doctrine in the field of public education. In *Cumming v. County Board of Education*, 175 U.S. 528 and *Gong Lum v. Rice*, 275 U.S. 78, the validity of the doctrine itself was challenged. In more recent cases, all on the graduate school level, inequality was found in that specific benefits enjoyed by white students ware denied to Negro students of the same educational qualifications. *Missouri ex rel. Gaines v. Canada*, 305 U.S. 337; *Sipuel v. Oklahoma*, 332 U.S. 631; *Sweatt v. Painter*, 339 U.S. 629; *McLaurin v. Oklahoma State Regents*, 339 U.S. 637. In none of these cases was it necessary to re-examine the doctrine to grant relief to the Negro plaintiff. And in *Sweat v. Painter, supra*, the Court expressly reserved decision on the question whether *Plessy v. Ferguson* should be inapplicable to public education.

In the instant cases, that question is directly presented. Here, unlike *Sweatt v. Painter*, there are findings below that the Negro and white schools involved have been equalized, or are being equalized, with respect to buildings, curricula, qualifications and salaries of teachers, and other "tangible" factors. Our decision, therefore, cannot turn on merely a comparison of these tangible factors in the Negro and white schools involved in each of the cases. We must look instead to the effect of segregation itself on public education.

In approaching this problem, we cannot turn the clock back to 1868 when the Amendment was adopted, or even to 1896 when *Plessy v. Ferguson*

son was written. We must consider public education in the light of its full development and its present place in American life throughout the Nation. Only in this way can it be determined if segregation in public schools deprives these plaintiffs of the equal protection of the laws.

Today, education is perhaps the most important function of state and local governments. Compulsory school attendance laws and the great expenditures for education both demonstrate our recognition of the importance of education to our democratic society. It is required in the performance of our most basic public responsibilities, even service in the armed forces. It is the very foundation of good citizenship. Today it is a principal instrument in awakening the child to cultural values, in preparing him for later professional training, and in helping him to adjust normally to his environment. In these days, it is doubtful that any child may reasonably be expected to succeed in life if he is denied the opportunity of an education. Such an opportunity, where the state has undertaken to provide it, is a right which must be made available to all on equal terms.

We come then to the question presented: Does segregation of children in public schools solely on the basis of race, even though the physical facilities and other "tangible" factors may be equal, deprive the children of the minority group of equal educational opportunities? We believe it does.

In *Sweatt v. Painter, supra,* in finding that a segregated law school for Negroes could not provide them equal educational opportunities, this Court relied in large part on "those qualities which are incapable of objective measurement but which make for greatness in a law school." *In McLaurin v. Oklahoma State Regents, supra,* the Court, in requiring that a Negro admitted to a white graduate school be treated like all other students, again resorted to intangible considerations: ". . . his ability to study, to engage in discussions and exchange views with other students, and, in general, to learn his profession." Such considerations apply with added force to children in grade and high schools. To separate them from others of similar age and qualifications solely because of their race generates a feeling of inferiority as to their status in the community that may affect their hearts and minds in a way unlikely ever to be undone. The effect of this separation on their educational opportunities was well stated by a finding in the Kansas case by a court which nevertheless felt compelled to rule against the Negro plaintiffs:

> "Segregation of white and colored children in public schools has a detrimental effect upon the colored children. The impact is greater when it has the sanction of the law; for the policy of separating the races is usually interpreted as denoting the inferiority of the negro group. A sense of inferiority affects the

> motivation of a child to learn. Segregation with the sanction of law, therefore, has a tendency to [retard] the educational and mental development of negro children and to deprive them of some of the benefits they would receive in a racial[ly] integrated school system."

Whatever may have been the extent of psychological knowledge at the time of *Plessy v. Ferguson*, this finding is amply supported by modern authority. Any language in *Plessy v. Ferguson*, contrary to this finding is rejected.

We conclude that in the field of public education the doctrine of "separate but equal" has no place. Separate educational facilities are inherently unequal. Therefore, we hold that the plaintiffs and others similarly situated for whom the actions have been brought are, by reason of the segregation complained of, deprived of the equal protection of the laws guaranteed by the Fourteenth Amendment. This disposition makes unnecessary any discussion whether such segregation also violates the Due Process Clause of the Fourteenth Amendment.

Because these are class actions, because of the wide applicability of this decision, and because of the great variety of local conditions, the formulation of decrees in these cases presents problems of considerable complexity. On reargument, the consideration of appropriate relief was necessarily subordinated to the primary question—the constitutionality of segregation in public education. We have now announced that such segregation is a denial of the equal protection of the laws. In order that we may have the full assistance of the parties in formulating decrees, the cases will be restored to the docket, and the parties are requested to present further argument on Questions 4 and 5 previously propounded by the Court for the reargument of this Term. The Attorney General of the United States is again invited to participate. The Attorneys General of the states requiring or permitting segregation in public education will also be permitted to appear as *amici curiae* upon request to do so by September 15, 1954, and submission of briefs by October 1, 1954.

It is so ordered.

SOURCE NOTES

Chapter 1

1. "Discussion of War Aims", The Annals Of America, (Encyclopaedia Britannica, 1976), vol. 9, p. 348.
2. "Civil War, U.S.", Encyclopaedia Britannica, Macropaedia, 15th ed., vol. 4, p. 681.
3. Peter M. Bergman, The Chronological History Of The Negro In America, (The New American Library, 1969), pp. 535-616 (for facts, events and occurrences of The Civil Rights Movement).
4. Esther Pessin, "New Racial Incident Reported in New York", UPI Article, The Middletown Press, Middletown, Connecticut, Dec. 24, 1986, p. 2.

Chapter 2

1. American Decisions, vol. 96, p. 614.
2. American Decisions, vol. 18, p. 54.
3. John Codman Hurd, The Law Of Freedom & Bondage In The United States, Vol. 2, (Baker & Godwin, Printers, 1862), pp. 1-218.
4. North Carolina Reports, vol 20, p. 503.
5. Gilbert Thomas Stephenson, Race Distinctions In American Law, (D. Appleton & Co. 1910), pp. 36-39.
6. United States Reports, vol. 60, p. 393.
7. Ibid., p. 423.
8. Ibid., p. 407.
9. United States Reports, vol. 109, p. 3.
10. Ibid., p. 14.
11. United States Reports, vol. 203, p. 1.
12. United States Reports, vol. 273, p. 536.
13. United States Reports, vol. 295, p. 45.
14. United States Reports, vol. 321, p. 663.
15. Harvard Law Review, Vol. 52, pp. 825-827.
16. United States Reports, vol. 163, p. 537.
17. Ibid., p. 550.
18. Ibid., pp. 551-552.
19. Ibid., p. 563.
20. Ibid., p. 557.

21. Pauli Murray, States' Laws On Race And Color, (Lit. Hdqr., Cincinnati, Ohio. 1950), pp. 14-18.
22. United States Reports, vol. 163, p. 537.
23. Atlantic Reporter, 2nd Series, Vol. 29, p. 253.
24. Atlantic Reporter, vol 192, p. 353.
25. Ibid., p. 355.
26. Ibid., p. 355.
27. United States Reports, vol. 305, p. 337.
28. United States Reports, vol. 332, p. 631.
29. United States Reports, vol. 339, p. 629.
30. Ibid., pp. 633-634.
31. Ibid., p. 637.
32. United States Reports, vol. 347, p. 483.
33. Ibid., p. 493.
34. Ibid., p. 495.
35. Federal Reporter, 2nd Series, vol. 220, p. 386.
36. Statistical Abstract Of The United States, 106th ed., (U.S. Dept. of Commerce, 1986).
37. "Poverty", Encyclopaedia Britannica, Macropaedia, 15th ed., vol. 14, pp. 935-940.

Chapter 3

1. United States Code Annotated, Title 42, Sections 2000a- 2000e.
2. For example, Connecticut General Statutes Annotated, Title 46a, Sections 52 & 82.
3. United States Code Annotated, Title 18, Section 241.
4. Ibid., Section 242.
5. For example, Connecticut General Statutes Annotated, Title 46a, Section 58; McKinney's Consolidated Laws of New York Annotated, Vol. 18, "Human Rights Law", Section 299.
6. Encyclopaedia of Associations, 24th Ed., Vol. 1, (Gale Research Co., 1990), Entries 7346, 7070 & 8095.
7. United States Code Annotated, Title 15, Sections 633 & 637.
8. For example, West's Annotated California Codes, Vol. 32B, "Government Code", Section 8850.3(d); Massachusetts General Laws Annotated, Vol. 2B, ch. 23A, Sections 39-44; Connecticut General Statutes Annotated, Title 32, Section 9n.
9. Encyclopaedia Of Associations, 24th Ed., Vol. 1, (Gale Research Co., 1990), Entries 13992, 13988 & 10978.
10. Ibid., Entries 5285, 5288, 5422 & 14261.
11. Ibid., Entries 15530 & 15527.
12. Stokley Carmichael, "What We Want", The Annals Of America, (Encyclopaedia Britannica, 1976), Vol. 18, pp. 373-380.

13. "Adams, John Quincy", Encyclopedia Britannica, Macropaedia, 15th ed., Vol. 1, pp. 78-80.

14. "Garrison, William Lloyd", Encyclopedia Britannica, Macropaedia, 15th ed., Vol. 7, p. 913.

15. Peter M. Bergman, The Chronological History Of The Negro In America, (The New American Library, 1969), p. 217.

16. Ibid., pp. 48-49.

17. Ibid., p. 138.

18. Ibid., p. 137.

19. Ibid., pp. 106-230; "United States, History Of The", Encyclopedia Britannica, Macropaedia, 15th ed., Vol. 18, pp. 960-971.

Chapter 4

1. "White Philadelphia Neighborhood Protests Arrival Of Black Families", Associated Press Article, The Hartford Courant, Hartford, Connecticut, Nov. 22, 1985, p. A4.

2. The New Republic, Feb. 9, 1987, p. 7.

3. "Group Claims Responsibility For Mail Bombs", Associated Press Article, The Middletown Press, Middletown, Connecticut, Dec. 29, 1989, p. 3.

4. American Jurisprudence, 2nd ed., Vol. 68, "Schools", Section 283.

5. West's Annotated California Codes, Vol. 28C, "Elections Code", Section 5353.

Chapter 5

1. Peter M. Bergman, The Chronological History Of The Negro In America, (The New American Library, 1969), p. 667.

2. Ibid., p. 668.

3. United States Reports, Vol. 438, p. 265.

4. United States Reports, Vol. 443, p. 193.

5. United States Reports, Vol. 478, p. 501.

6. United States Reports, Vol. 480, p. 149.

7. United States Reports, Vol. 467, p. 561.

8. For example of attitudes, see Juan Williams, "White Amnesia About '50 Civil Rights Movement", The Hartford Courant, Hartford, Connecticut, March 7, 1987, pp. C1 & C4.

Index

A

B

C

D

E

F

G

H

I

J

K

L

M

N

O

P

Q

R